the

touchstone
TOOLS

ALSO BY JOSEPH HOLLAND

From Harlem with Love: An Ivy Leaguer's Inner City Odyssey

Holistic Hardware: Tools That Build Lives—THE VIDEO SERIES

the touchstone TOOLS

Building Your Way
to an
Inspired Life

JOSEPH HOLLAND

GRAND
HARBOR
PRESS

AUTHOR'S NOTE: The stories in this book were composed from memory without additional research, and the names and identities of the characters have been altered to protect privacy.

Published by Grand Harbor Press, Grand Haven

www.brilliancepublishing.com

Amazon, the Amazon logo, and Grand Harbor Press are trademarks of Amazon.com, Inc., or its affiliates.

ISBN-13: 9781503945418
ISBN-10: 1503945413

Cover design by: Tim Green, Faceout Studio

Printed in the United States of America

To my children
Shelby, Jason and Laura

May the tools of this book inspire you
to soar beyond the storms.

CONTENTS

INTRODUCTION
THE MISSING TOOLBOX

*If my only tool is a hammer, then all my problems will look
like nails.*

—*Mark Twain*

It all began with Henry, on a crack cocaine–captured street corner in
the heart of Harlem. Drugs, crime, and flight had turned Harlem of
the early eighties into an urban wasteland where abandoned buildings
blighted the streetscape like potholes on a winter-ravaged roadway.

Henry was a regular at the outreach forays of Harlem's Ark of Free-
dom, the nonprofit I founded, offering food and clothing in front of
vacant buildings and empty lots. I was drawn by his radar-like persistence (he always seemed to find us, week after week, no matter how forlorn our venue) as well as by his peppy mood, bright smile, and quick
wit ("You bringin' me steak next time, righ'?")—all of which belied his
dreary circumstances.

Homeless, hungry, hurting, Henry was a generational archetype
of the inner city; the progeny of generations who'd had their dreams
deferred. His grandparents had fled the Jim Crow South for the promised land of the Harlem Renaissance, only to be confounded by the
Great Depression and the deplorable housing, limited and poor

educational opportunities, pervasive unemployment, and irrepressible racism in its wake.

Henry's teenage mom raised him and his horde of siblings in a couple of Harlem's plethora of public housing projects, known more for gangbanging than ghetto-busting. He dropped out of school and left home, taking flight with nowhere to go but down into a purgatory of soup kitchens, homeless shelters, and crack dens. It took me too long to realize that Henry needed more than the hearty sandwiches, passionate preaching, winter coats, and gospel singing that my charity provided.

By then he'd stopped showing up, so I went looking for him at his "residence"—the Harlem armory shelter. I didn't find him, but discovered hundreds of Henrys in a sea of cots adrift across the drill hall floor. I watched the staff drag men out of bed, giving up my search when guns were brandished in a fight over a broken crack-pipe stem. I fled the scene. I never saw Henry again.

I lamented my inability to fundamentally help Henry, blaming my eclectic background, which left me feeling—initially, at least—ill equipped to uplift the Henrys of Harlem. Growing up as an African American in the 1960s South, the civil rights movement was a defining experience. Marches, protests, and sit-ins made social justice the order of the day. An ethos pervaded this period that progress for the disadvantaged and disenfranchised was a real possibility.

I moved from the civil rights South of the sixties to an itinerant life in the seventies: a Scandinavian sojourn with my diplomat dad, then to the suburban Northeast US for high school and the Ivy League for college and law school. I retained my values around rectifying racial injustice, which were strengthened when I became a devout Christian in my early twenties, learning to live the Biblical precept "To whom much is given, much is required." The confluence of cultural consciousness and spiritual calling motivated me upon graduating law school to relocate from Harvard to Harlem, stepping from the esoteric arguments of the ivory tower to unadorned truths at the grassroots level.

But once in Harlem, with the best of intentions, I kept leading my outreach group into burned-out blocks with Henry-like outcomes. There had to be a better way, I thought, than our earnest but ineffectual efforts and the monolithic city shelter masquerading as Henry's way station. No one at that shelter, it seemed, was acknowledging his humanity. No one was dealing with his uniqueness as an individual. No one was even trying to confront the poverty of spirit that gave rise to his material destitution. Henry had received "three hots and a cot" but nothing more.

But I, too, had been failing the Henrys of Harlem. They gladly received street outreach provisions, but these offerings weren't enough to turn them away from chronic crisis to permanent progress. Transforming their lives would be impossible as long as they remained in the underworld of urban streets and uncaring shelters.

Resolved to create a physical and moral environment to uplift the Henrys of Harlem, I started Harkhomes, a "home" for fifteen homeless men in a Harlem church basement. My vision was holistic housing: shelter not as an end in itself but as a means to restore the whole person. I wanted the place to go beyond the material basics to provide hope, purpose, family—the stuff out of which lives are transformed. With no budget but lots of faith, I recruited male volunteers from the outreach group to supervise the residents each night and to mentor them toward a better way.

From the very first night, long lines formed outside for the first-come-first-served beds. The demand was encouraging, but the results weren't. Throughout the first few months of feeding and chastising and clothing and preaching and counseling and praying, the Henrys of Harlem came and went, as if I simply moved them, like the deck chairs on the *Titanic*, from one futile circumstance to another. The church landlord became so frustrated with the revolving-door atmosphere that Harkhomes was evicted: my homeless shelter itself became homeless. Fortunately, though, not for long—a second chance came in a church basement on a neighboring block.

During the first week in our new home, sleepless over the incessant struggles at the shelter, fasting and praying for what to do, a revelation came: *Begin each day with Bible study.* Since I wasn't sure how to sow seeds of progress for my challenged residents, searching the Scriptures seemed my best hope of finding some fertile ground.

The very next morning, I gathered the fifteen residents together in the Fellowship Room—before breakfast, to the aggravation of all. Not sure where to focus, I started with my favorite New Testament passage from the Sermon on the Mount—Jesus's parable of the two houses—reciting the text: "The rain came down, the streams rose, and the winds blew and beat against that house; yet it did not fall, because it had its foundation on the rock" (Matthew 7:25).

"Jesus compares your life to houses in a storm: wind, rain, floods beating against two houses," I paraphrased, too tired for exhortation. "The house built on sand collapses, buffeted by the storm," I continued. "But the house built on rock remains standing."

"I'm like that first house—the one collapsing," exclaimed Spike, an unsurprising confession given his reckless habits. "Whenever there's trouble, I just fall apart." His confession sparked a chorus of affirmations from the weary men sitting around the table.

"I keep going down when crisis comes" . . . "I got blown away again last week" . . . "Forget about that sand. I feel like I'm stuck in quicksand" . . . "Made a mess out of my life" . . . "I've been rained out for a pretty long time."

Capitalizing on what I expected to be but a moment of collective attentiveness, I quickly connected the dots. "The point of the parable is that the houses stand or fall based on their foundation. You will stand or fall, crash or soar, based on your foundational principles. The virtues you possess on the inside are more important than the crises raging on the outside. The values of life determine the success of life!" I exclaimed, finally finding a preacher's rhythm.

Taking a long breath to let the last point linger, I observed that no one was falling asleep—not even Ray, whom I'd nicknamed Ray Van Winkle, since he was forever nodding off.

"You will make it through the storms of life if you forge a positive attitude and cultivate a strong character." Energized, I stood. "To make it through the storms of life and to build your personal house of progress that will not fall, you need to use the right tools!"

"Where's my toolbox?"

Ray's question ignited the room. A chorus of "I need tools, too" rang out like "amens."

As I closed the session in prayer, launching the mad rush for breakfast, Ray's query lingered like the inner-city gloom that haunted the Henrys of Harlem. Where was this *toolbox*?

My mind rang with possibility, exploring the metaphorical landscape. What if Ray was like a broken-down house, lacking a solid moral foundation and overcome by the storms of life, needing more than a minor repair here and a patch up there, but the heavy duty *tools* that would enable him to demolish the ruin and construct a new life in its place?

I discreetly studied Ray as he consumed his second plateful of grits and eggs. The food helped, as did his cot and hand-me-down jeans, as would the GED classes and AA meetings if he would ever show up for them. But he needed and wanted something more, something deeper than the needs of the body to lift the soul and spirit.

Watching him and his peers jockey over the scraps and crumbs, it struck me that they were vying for the wrong things. To really make a difference, to overcome, to be transformed and inspired, it was a spiritual thing—an inner journey on which they could reach down within themselves and build a sturdy framework of principles, values, and disciplines that would yield both sound decision making and serious destiny seeking.

In that moment, I was anointed for a new mission: gathering the philosophies, actions, and tenets that would serve as touchstones for Ray's toolbox.

And so began my quest that transformed Harkhomes into a "social workshop" where these touchstone tools were invented, implemented, and refined. I discovered that a regular diet of principles and disciplines fostered moral fortitude in the same way that supplying food, clothing, and shelter sustained physical strength.

Day by day, week after week, by trial-and-error, the tools evolved into a remedial *and* preventative regimen of spiritual values, practical strategies, high expectations, principle-centered life skills, and an ethic of personal responsibility. Often to my surprise and always to my delight, the tools worked. Over a dozen years I witnessed how the hundreds of Harkhomes men responded to the question "What's in your toolbox?"—which proved to be the critical factor as to why some were able to better their circumstances and change their destiny and others weren't.

The tools lived beyond Harkhomes through my work as a motivational speaker, parent, and community-based entrepreneur, as well as through Holistic Hardware—a curriculum-based series of videos and workshops I developed. The toolbox matured into more than a resource for those in dire straits, but, just as important, also for those seeking to triumph over everyday challenges. After all, tools that fix broken-down vehicles work just as well on cars that need only a tune-up. This book chronicles the emergence and efficacy of the toolbox, and the lives that were transformed as a result, including my own.

Whether you are facing setbacks and adversities, feeling overwhelmed and lost, or simply living beneath your God-given potential and seeking more meaning out of life, these are the tools that will fortify you with a moral core, spiritual fiber, inner vitality, and insightful strategies to build your way to an inspired life.

Just like a mechanic using a manual in his workshop or a carpenter following a blueprint on site, this book will help you know when to use the hammer of discipline, or the shovel of responsibility, or the binoculars of vision, or the drill of faith, or the lift of love. Technique *and* timing are key in using these and the other tools. You will find that their power lies in how easily and readily you can pull the right principle out of the toolbox of your consciousness and use it to your advantage in the midst of the present predicament.

Each chapter helps you activate the tools in three ways:

- **Learning the tools.** I describe, as the substance of each chapter, the genesis of each tool and how it had a tangible, positive impact on the lives of people who embraced and employed it. These unforgettable stories of transformation are offered to inspire you and to illustrate the holistic dynamic—the spirit-soul-body perspective—that is at the heart of the tools. If you believe differently about your situation (spirit as renewed faith), you will think differently about it (soul as renewed attitude), then you will act differently—and victoriously (body as renewed lifestyle). And a big part of learning the tools is passing them on. Sharing these stories with others will demonstrate how well you have embraced their meaning for yourself; imparting them will also be a source of inspiration for your listeners.

- **Sharpening the tools.** After the storyline comes the sharpening. The tools will do you no good if they remain only words on a page rather than principles at work in your life. To make the tools user-friendly, five tips for applying them conclude each chapter, challenging you to take concrete steps to implement these *touchstones* on a daily basis. Living out the tools in this way will encourage you to manifest this inner journey of renewal as a lifestyle.

- **Affirming the tools.** After the honing comes the polishing. Affirming the tools means committing the key principles to memory and confessing their truth to yourself and others to release their power. Say them aloud and/or write them down for constant reinforcement. The key is to rehearse these words each day, early and often—intentionally, again and again, until they become second nature.

So here's your three-step personal inspirational plan:

LEARN THE TOOLS

DO THE STEPS

SAY THE AFFIRMATIONS

If you use the tools in these ways—each of the three actions is important in its own way—you will build inspiration into your life.

But please understand: the tools, as you apply them, will not provide a specific mathematical formula to living the inspired life. However, they will alter your perceptions of the challenges you face and the solutions that are appropriate. Utilizing them is not clear, precise, or cut-and-dried, but rather random, spontaneous, or even haphazard and messy—because that's the way you are. Human nature is more art than science, more about the real stuff in your lifestyle for which you need the tools than the theoretical stuff in your mind that's been keeping you from taking action. Your life is complex, which is why there are ten tools—to fit you where you are. It is a deeply personal quest—what you need to change, or adjust about yourself, or your attitudes in order to get where you want to go.

Finally, you must also understand that the *toolbox* is not a quick fix; the *touchstones* are not a panacea guaranteeing perfect solutions or speedy results. The *tools* are proven effective if you commit to their regular use. And they respond best to your determination and devotion—and to your faith. Though the tools are practical in effect, they are spiritual in nature: the whole is greater than the sum of their parts. When using them, expect the unexpected, the serendipitous, the providential. The solution that unfolds may not be the one that you had in mind, but the mystery of the miraculous may take you to higher ground of divine outcomes, far different from *and* far better than anything you could have or would have imagined.

Are you ready?

TOOL #1

RESPONSIBILITY
THE TUDE
BUILDING POSITIVE ATTITUDE

Another early morning at Harkhomes, the men gathered for the daily fellowship and devotion that started the day. I stuck with the spiritual routine, but I decided to lay off Scripture, which, I'd hoped, would quiet the complainers ("Why you always so preachy, Rev?") and stir some of the sleepyheads whose snoring seemed to crescendo whenever I opened the Bible. So I floated a favorite maxim.

"If you give a man a fish, he'll eat for a day." I paused as a couple of pairs of eyes brightened at the good news, but the gregarious Slim also perked up, which wasn't good news. I wasn't in the mood for commentary from the resident loudmouth.

I pressed on—"If you teach him how to fish"—hoping to beat him to the punch line. Wishful thinking. Before I could utter the telling words "he'll eat for a lifetime," Slim cut me off with his coup de grace: "He'll sit in a boat drinking beer all day!"

The room erupted in laughter. Not at all amused, I raised my voice to inject the correct line but lost again to the quick-witted Slim, who fired another zinger: "You give him something to do while he waits for his government check."

Their laughter was a not so funny reminder of my Sisyphean endeavor. I adjourned for breakfast.

Take Ownership

Lawrence was the only one not laughing that morning, which was no surprise given his dour demeanor. He'd come to Harkhomes from a park bench in nearby Marcus Garvey Park. The typical intake process was first-come-first-served off the long line of hopefuls waiting outside every night for an available bed. But Lawrence got in through the back door, so to speak, via the "Jesus Hunters."

Inspired by Jesus's words—"I was a stranger and you invited me in"—this group of self-motivated Harkhomes residents hit the streets whenever a bed was empty with the mission of "hunting for strangers like Jesus" who they could invite to take the empty bed. Lawrence was so weak that the hunters carried him the five blocks from park to shelter.

His caustic countenance made Lawrence the most unapproachable of the current crowd, but I ventured an icebreaker later that day. "You ever been fishing?" I asked as he halfheartedly mopped the bathroom floor.

Lawrence indignantly stared me down. "I'm a black man in America," he fired at me, as if the answer were obvious. "I don't do fishing. I'm the one on the hook."

I studied him for a moment, pondering whether to probe or punt. I decided to risk it.

"You must avoid using the legacies of slavery and racism as an ever-ready rationale for personal shortcomings," I asserted, aware of my tendency—my Harlem learning curve having been quite steep—of using an Ivy League argument for an inner-city conundrum.

In the verbal onslaught that ensued, Lawrence covered the spectrum of his racial difficulty. He bought his first drugs from a "white pusher," lost a fortune when he was swindled by a "white hustler," and got arrested when he was hoodwinked by a "white mole."

When I cautioned him against making Caucasians his favorite scapegoats, he exploded with a new round of complaints.

"We're always the last hired and the first fired." He'd lost his job because his foreman was a racist; of course, it had nothing to do his raging temper and the fight where he knocked out a white coworker.

Tiring of his tirade, I lost my temper. "Wake up! The problems of too many people are always someone else's fault. People blame God, kids blame parents, wives blame husbands, husbands blame wives, and you blame the white man. Grow up and take some responsibility for your own problems!"

It was as if he hadn't heard me.

"There's a conspiracy to emasculate the black man." He'd lost his apartment because he was black and the landlord was white; of course, it had nothing to do with the fact that he had not paid rent in six months.

"Hating white folks won't solve your plight."

"I don't hate white folks. It's just wrong that they been hatin' on black folks since the Middle Passage!"

He stormed off, which confirmed my sense of the destructive emotions and pathology simmering inside him. I'd already learned in my couple of years running Harkhomes that homelessness was most often a symptom of deeper, complex issues, difficulties that Lawrence—stuck in his racial morass—never addressed . . . or even realized.

The next day, Lawrence informed me that he was leaving Harkhomes, which I attributed, in large part, to my arguing with him. Anguished, I resolved to take another shot at getting him to consider an introspective approach: to honestly assess his own flaws and shortcomings and to eschew the burdens of racism which acted as blinders, keeping him focused on others and preventing him from looking within to discern the personal dimensions of his plight.

This time I avoided adages and especially the racial hot button. Instead, I shared a personal experience, a seminal moment when as a preteen I first really learned about responsibility.

I told him about my first summer job in the college library on the campus of Hampton University, where my father was president. Shelving books, packing dated materials for storage, sorting and filing newspapers and magazines, and keeping the reading room in order, I worked for the head librarian, who ruled her domain with an iron fist.

An avid sports fan, I would pore through the back issues of the library's collection of sports magazines, which broke the monotony of my tasks. Since there was never enough time to read about all my favorite teams and players in the stacks of magazines, I "borrowed" them on a daily basis, stuffing the mostly out-of-date periodicals in my gym bag to continue reading at home, intending to return them, but never quite getting around to it.

One day near the end of my shift, I was sorting through some magazines, slipping the ones I had decided to take home into my bag, when my boss caught me red-handed. I quickly and nervously stammered off a litany of excuses, even desperately pointing the finger at the assistant librarian for not supervising my behavior.

"What's the point?" Lawrence had lost patience, which I should've expected with this protracted biographical account.

"This is what she told me," I said, rushing to the conclusion. "'The only thing worse than making excuses is to blame someone else for your own shortcomings. Accepting your role in causing the problem is like taking ownership of it; then you can take on the responsibility of straightening it out. You must own it. If you don't own it, you won't fix it.'"

Lawrence seemed pensive, raising my hopes for a breakthrough, so I soldiered on. "She concluded with the key point: 'Think of your life as journey. You're on a train moving toward a destination called success. Refusing to take ownership and blaming others—that's a big threat to derail your train.'"

He made a perfunctory remark about how there were more black men in prison than in college and walked away. My efforts to tame his anger had proven fruitless. I felt like a teacher going back to the drawing board with no chalk.

Not long thereafter, Lawrence moved out of Harkhomes and into his cousin's apartment. Since his cousin was a known drug dealer, I knew where this was going, but the outcome was worse than expected. A drug deal went bad. The cousin fled town with the money. The drug suppliers broke into the apartment with guns drawn. Lawrence fled out the window, dodging bullets as he bolted down the fire escape and through the alleyway.

On one of their forays, the Jesus Hunters discovered that Lawrence was hiding out in the 8th Avenue subway tunnel. I asked them to take me there. What was I thinking? Rats as big as cats trampled my feet. The nauseating odor of garbage and heaven knows what else flared my nostrils. Rodent feces clung to my sneaker heel. I hoped we couldn't find him so I could escape this horror as soon as possible.

I passed the flashlight and pinched my nose to keep from turning back.

Soon enough we came upon Lawrence, sitting on a crumpled trash can, obscured by shadows. I handed him dinner leftovers, and he ravaged a chicken breast. Still stuck in the rut of his blamefulness, he launched into a tirade against his "double-crossing cousin." I cut him off. I'd journeyed with increasing reluctance to this God-forsaken place, having lost my patience along the way.

"Do you know Jesus's parable of the prodigal son?" I asked him.

"The one who ran away from home?"

"And ended up homeless and hungry, foraging for food in a pigsty. Remind you of anyone you know?" He looked away, then back at me. Our eyes locked.

"What did the prodigal son do?" he asked with surprising earnestness.

"He honestly assessed his situation. He said to himself, 'My father's servants have more than enough to eat, and here I am starving to death.' In other words, he asked himself, 'How did I wind up in such a mess?' His inner journey led to his decision to leave his desperate circumstances and return home."

"Does this mean I can come back to Harkhomes?"

"And leave all your four-legged friends behind?" I said, waving my hand at the rats running to and fro. I should've expected my attempt at levity to fall flat given his sourpuss personality. Though he didn't crack a smile, neither did he make a comment about the white rats persecuting the black rats. And I sensed in his question not just the desperation of a man at rock bottom, but something new, different, perhaps an openness to change. Maybe I was reading too much into it, but the sooner I went for the jugular, the sooner I could get out of this hellhole.

"Are you ready to stop blaming others and start taking responsibility?"

He stared at me blankly, then hung his head. I looked around. A mountain of rat manure caught my attention, resurrecting a favorite parable.

"A father had twin ten-year-old sons. The sons were identical in appearance but opposite in attitude: one was always positive, the other was always negative, so much so that the father decided to call in a psychiatrist to examine them. The shrink set up a test. He put the negative son in a room full of toys, gadgets, and playthings, and the positive son in a room full of horse manure."

I took a moment to scrape some rat manure from the bottom of my sneakers, to highlight the point. I waited for Lawrence's "What's the point?" but nothing came forth. He only grimaced as the dung fell to the ground, letting me know he was listening.

"An hour later, the father and the shrink went to check on the boys. They found the negative son crying; he said to his father, 'Why did you put all these nice things in here? You knew I'd break them. I didn't touch anything.' But they found the positive son having a great time, playing, throwing, swimming, and diving in the manure, exclaiming as he came up for air, 'There's so much manure, there has to be a pony in here somewhere!'"

Lawrence chuckled; it was a nervous chuckle, but it was the first time I'd ever heard him laugh.

"What ya saying, Rev? My Tude stinks?"

"Your what?"

"My Tude—'hood talk for 'attitude,'" he explained.

"Well, yes. You're the first kid—blaming others, always complaining about things. Be like the second kid. Take ownership of your manure, no matter how bad it smells. Work through your stuff with a positive attitude. Don't look for the problem, look for the pony."

"Does that mean there's a good white man out there somewhere?"

"With a new Tude," I affirmed, "you will find a lot of them."

He paused, pensive, for what seemed like an eternity. The scurrying of rodents was the only thing that broke the silence.

"Everything that happens to me is not the white man's fault," he declared after a moment, as if the realization was just sinking in.

In the noisome nook of an underground tunnel, Lawrence's inner journey to responsibility had begun.

We climbed out of there—finally!—and walked together in silence, with the Jesus Hunters as our protective posse, back to Harkhomes.

Lawrence's road to responsibility was rocky. He vacillated between reticence and anger, defiance and humility, self-righteousness and repentance. It was a different Lawrence every day, sometimes every hour of a day. At one point he decided to talk as little as possible because whatever came out of his mouth was the same old negative, accusatory statements. He'd become a high-maintenance resident, requiring continual correction and counseling. After months of sorting through his cynical thoughts and feelings, he'd discarded practically all of them.

The breakthrough happened when he stood before his fellow residents after the evening meal and acknowledged his prejudice. It was as if he was throwing off the shackles of hatred, freeing him to perceive the truth of others, and accept them without bias.

Lawrence resolved to read the Bible from cover to cover to cultivate a new mindset. It helped so much that he read it again, and again, memorizing key verses, until his thinking felt renewed. Convinced that education was his destiny, he secured his GED, then gained admittance to a community college, working part time around his class schedule as a waiter at a midtown restaurant, with the goal of becoming a high school history teacher emphasizing African American culture.

His favorite college professor, who became his mentor, was a white man.

Take Initiative

Slim, the Harkhomes comedian, observed with great interest the changes in Lawrence. His joke about Lawrence was a house favorite: "Why did Lawrence marry a white woman and make her wear white at the wedding? Because he wanted his dishwasher to match his fridge and oven." But with Lawrence's new Tude, Slim's jokes became passé.

A thirtysomething African American, Slim seemed to have zero body fat, thus his well-earned nickname. But despite his stature and nickname, he displayed the insatiable appetite of an NFL lineman at every meal.

His sense of humor was incorrigible. When I asked him how he lost his job as a shipping clerk, he quipped: "What's the difference between Bigfoot and an intelligent boss? There have actually been sightings of Bigfoot." I feigned a chuckle, concerned that he was always hiding behind his jokes, using humor as deflection.

Slim was quick to attribute his problems to the two women in his life: his mother and his wife. "Mom didn't like work and she wasn't too bright," he told me. "When her sister visited our apartment and tore down the cobwebs, Mom screamed, 'Who's messing with my drapes?'"

Slim described ongoing, intensifying domestic strife, giving graphic detail about arguments with his wife, especially the climactic one that ended with her putting him out. "She wanted to go someplace for her birthday that she hadn't been for a long time," Slim recounted. "I said to her, 'What about the kitchen?'" She changed the locks the next day.

I probed, sensing something more than overreaction to an ill-timed joke. But Slim stuck to his story, blaming an unsupportive wife. "It's not my problem, it's her," he said defiantly.

"Well, you're the one who's homeless now, so it *is* your problem," I countered.

"Maybe you should pray that she forgives me."

His sarcastic retort triggered a Biblical reference from me. "Why do you look at the speck of sawdust in your brother's eye and pay no attention to the plank in your own eye?"

"What?" At least I'd disarmed his sense of humor.

I explained to Slim that when Jesus asked this rhetorical question, he was challenging his listeners to look inward to get in touch with their own flaws and shortcomings before pointing the finger of blame at others. Recalling my counsel to Lawrence, I reminded him, "Don't put it all on your wife. Own it so you can fix it."

Slim gave a perfunctory nod and reaffirmed his overbearing wife as the reason for his plight.

"Where's your Tude?" I challenged him.

"Is 'Tude' the only Lenox Ave lingo you know?" he laughed.

Though he ignored my spiritual counsel, he did heed my advice about restoring his employment. With a "new" wardrobe acquired from a church clothing ministry and retooled employment interview skills through a job-training workshop, Slim was rehired at his old job.

Concerned that he was more focused on his outer than inner journey, I confronted him one morning as he dressed for work. "You remember my King David principle," I said, referring to a recent morning teaching on responsibility.

"Beware of bathing beauties," he comically recalled the turning point of the Old Testament passage, when David observed Bathsheba bathing on a rooftop and fell to temptation.

"Actually, it's 'Don't jump from the frying pan into the fire,'" I said, reminding him of the key principle from the biblical account.

After having discovered that Bathsheba had become pregnant from their adulterous encounter, King David ordered his general to send her husband, Uriah, into battle, then to pull back the troops, ensuring Uriah's death. So David went from adulterer to murderer, leading to a reign of terror on himself and his family.

Surprisingly, Slim had nothing funny to say. He finished dressing for work without uttering a word. Had I struck a nerve?

Fed up with my sermonettes—he riffed about my "24/7 preaching"—he initiated a "make nice" campaign with his wife, appointing a portion of each paycheck toward sending her flowers, contributing to the rent, and helping out with other household expenses and the kids' school supplies. Slim also called her every day. After four months at Harkhomes, Slim moved back home.

Just a week after having moved out, Slim was back, late at night, knocking on the Harkhomes door. I was asleep on my hallway cot, positioned so that there could be no predawn escapees. Though we had an empty bed that night, I decided to sleep through his banging. After all, I knew what had likely happened—another blowout with his wife. But the banging and implorations—"Open up, Rev, it's Slim!"—soon became too incessant to ignore.

I cracked the door. "Where's Slim? You look like King David to me." I slammed the door in his face.

His pleading persisted. I waited, long enough for my point to sink in. I opened the door a little wider this time.

"I'm sorry, Rev. All I need is a second chance," he begged. "Got to tell you something."

I leaned toward him. His vodka breath stung my nostrils. "Tell me what?"

"I'm ready to take the plank out of my eye," he said with conviction.

I could tell he wasn't joking.

I opened the door.

Slim and I talked until dawn. He'd been living a lie for a long time, wearing a mask of chuckles and grins. "I'm a gambler," he confessed. "And I'm an alcoholic, too."

For years he'd been slipping away from his job at lunch and scurrying around after work, stealing time for a card game, slot machine, or dice throw wherever he could, concealing his habit from his family. His wife had finally busted him—short on the rent money one too many times—and put him out of the house, landing him at Harkhomes the first time around.

Since Slim was in denial, not once did he mention anything about his problem with gambling and drinking during this initial stint. A master of deceit through those months at the shelter, whenever he got the chance, he would sneak out and hang out with his gambling buddies.

Slim fooled me but not his wife, who sensed that nothing important had changed upon his return home. She enlisted her brother to follow Slim after work one day; an incriminating photo was taken and presented to the suspicious spouse and Slim was back out on the streets within a week of his homecoming.

During our conversation that night, I returned to my early library lesson that had initially bombed with Lawrence. (Hope springs eternal.) My librarian boss not only required that I take ownership of my "borrowing" problem, I related to Slim. She also demanded that I take initiative.

"Put those magazines back, exactly in the places where you found them," she had ordered after discovering the periodicals in my gym bag. "And bring whatever else you've taken home back to the library, and don't you dare take another item out of here. Or would you like for me to enlist the help of President Holland to ensure the return of your 'borrowed' items?"

I assured her that that wouldn't be necessary.

"So what did you do?" Slim asked

"I took the initiative," I declared, relieved that Slim had responded better to my trip down memory lane than Lawrence. "I did what she said, working the rest of the summer reading only what I could on the job. But I didn't have much time for reading with all the extra work she assigned me to 'repair the damage caused by your irresponsibility.' I had to do it to keep from going from bad to worse—a tougher job to no job at all."

"Like me," he affirmed.

"And like your buddy Lawrence, who, before his turnaround, went from bad to worse, from being a homeless man to a homeless fugitive, running for his life."

"Not sure which is worse," he smirked, "running for your life or running from your wife."

Even in the wee hours, his sense of humor was tireless. I didn't mind his wisecracks so much anymore because his Tude changed—he took both ownership and initiative. He acknowledged his gambling problem, which was the crucial step—but only the first one—on his inward trek toward a responsible lifestyle. This stepping-stone of honest assessment took him to a deeper place—the dark corner within, where the accomplice of alcoholism lurked. He always gambled when he drank and he always drank when he gambled. The vices went hand in hand; he couldn't fix one without overhauling the other.

Every day I challenged him—"Where's your Tude?"—as he struggled to make it to AA meetings instead of the gambling hole and his favorite bar. His inconsistency compelled me to assign a fellow Harkhomes resident as a shadow; he grudgingly agreed to have a partner accompany him as an accountability factor whenever he left the shelter.

A year of painstaking ownership and initiative later, with a new Tude and a new job on Slim's part, his wife was ready to give him another chance. However, she had several conditions before she would allow him to return home. Of course, there would be no gambling or drinking, but she also had two new requirements: he would have to start attending church with her, and she would have exclusive control over the family finances.

In the past Slim would have rebelled, complaining about her domineering ways. Now he joked about it. "What's the definition of a mixed emotion?" he asked the brothers over dinner on his last night at Harkhomes. My lousy sense of humor precluded me from even a guess, but Cool Breeze jumped all over it—"Watching your mother-in-law reverse off a cliff while driving your brand-new car."

"That's the old answer," Slim chuckled.

"What's the new one?" Cool Breeze and the rest of us wondered.

"Leaving my Harkhomes family for my wife and kids."

Later that night, Slim observed my careworn expression after turning away another wayward soul.

"Where's your Tude, Rev?" he asked me. "Up or down?" He flashed the thumbs-up at me. Smiling, I returned it.

"Remember that guy King David?" he asked.

"Yes. Why?" I had no idea what was coming, but was pleased that a scriptural illustration of so long ago had stuck and was coming back as a punch line.

"Poor guy. I left him on the fishing boat drinking beer."

We shared a laugh.

"But there's hope for him," he assured me.

"For King David?" I played along as his set up man.

"If you teach him how to fish with the new Tude," Slim proclaimed, "he'll own the lake someday."

Sharpen Your Tools

The true meaning of responsibility is expressed in the word itself: it is the *ability* to *respond* effectively to the situations of life. The *responsibility tool* compels you to accept the role you played to create your present circumstances, which in turn prepares you mentally and emotionally to change them for the better. Follow these steps to build greater responsibility into your life and to own and shape your future.

Step one: Own your shortcomings. Be honest about your weaknesses. Admit your mistakes. Take the plank out of your own eye. Shift the focus from external factors—people, places, and things that were formerly the objects of blame—to where it fundamentally belongs: on you. Be transparent about your shortcomings to yourself and others. Are you selfish? Insecure? Arrogant? Lazy? Hardhearted? "No, not me," you might say. Take a deeper look. Sometimes the pathway to your inner truth can be as simple as asking yourself, "Why am I in this situation?" Whatever attitude or behavior got you there—identify it. Confess it. Own it. That's the first step to moving beyond it.

Step two: Open a new door. After you own it, it's time to do something about it. There will be times when you're not sure what to do next. Don't let that uncertainty keep you from doing *something*. Doing the usual—watching TV, speculating about the possibilities, listening to music, chatting on the phone, deliberating over options, or hanging out with your friends—will not resolve your issues. Be bold. Take the initiative. Try a different approach. Open a new door. If it's locked, go to the next door and try it. If it's the wrong room, don't go in. Don't jump from the frying pan into the fire; just keep it moving. If you're going to do something worthwhile with your life, you will have to take some risks. Taking ownership as you take initiative will help you manage those risks.

Step three: Optimize your attitude. Where's your Tude? Take responsibility for it and keep checking in on it throughout your day. Remember—the only constant in life is change. Your plans sometimes shift, strategies fail, timelines lengthen, people disappoint, resources run out, storms blow in, assumptions prove false. Refuse to allow changes and challenges to derail your positive attitude. Attitude determines approach. And your approach determines success or failure. Is your Tude up or down? Positive or negative? Keep your Tude up. If it's high enough, your mood, your outlook, your energy will stay strong, preparing you for whatever obstacles come your way, no matter how formidable they might be or bad they might smell. Think that you can make it happen, and your Tude will change from enemy to friend.

Step four: Override your pride. We live in the season of the selfie. The culture of social media says promote yourself; tell the world how wonderful you are; after all, it's all about you. Take a breather from the social media mania that insists everything is about *you*. Push pride to the side. Take the spotlight off yourself. Are you full of your own words, or are you listening well? Are you preoccupied with what the world can do for you, or have you given any thought about what you can offer the world? Acknowledge that you still have much to learn from life and from others. Look after the interests of others before your own. Make humility a part of your outlook. You will become more emotionally and spiritually healthy.

Step five: Offer your best. You are responsible for your inner life, for making the effort to improve yourself, to delve deeper into your truth, to step up to higher ground. You will reap what you sow. If you go through life half-stepping, you will never hit full stride. Don't build your life aiming to be better than others. Build your life to be better than you used to be, to be the best you can possibly be. Commit to that better you, whatever it takes. That is your greatest responsibility.

YOUR RESPONSIBILITY AFFIRMATION

I will take ownership of my situation, honestly assessing the wrong choices I have made, and I will take the initiative to correct the consequences of those choices, learning lessons so they will never happen again.

TOOL #2
VISION
THE PICTURE
BUILDING SELF-MOTIVATION

Each night at Harkhomes, I typically reviewed the morning scriptural lesson before offering a blessing over the evening meal, undeterred by the impatience of the diners—some with fork in hand. I established this routine as yet another way to reinforce the tools. But tonight I decided to leaven the biblical with the literary, hoping to defuse their carping— "Another scripture, Rev?!" Wishful thinking was one of the habits I was hoping to curb.

I quickly summarized the biblical story we'd discussed that morning, that of Joseph, the Old Testament figure who possessed soaring dreams for his life. He saw a vision of the harvest, with his sheaf rising above the sheaves of his eleven brothers; and a vision of the heavens, with his sun rising above the stars of his family members.

My setup complete, anticipating my subject the next morning, I asked the men, "What happens to a dream deferred?"

It was a rhetorical question. I paused briefly for emphasis, intending to recite the rest of the Langston Hughes poem "Harlem." But before I could say the next line, I heard a voice.

"Like a raisin in the sun, it dries up," Arthur whispered, as if he didn't want to be heard.

I was stunned that a Harkhomes man was quoting a Harlem Renaissance poet. What made the moment especially incredulous was that the words came from Arthur, who was always the last one out of bed in the morning and wouldn't recognize motivation if it walked up and slapped him in the face.

"What did you say, Arthur?" I asked.

"Nothing, never mind," Arthur said dismissively.

"It was something about a raisin getting a suntan," offered Ray, who had recently returned for another Harkhomes tour of duty.

"Can we eat now, Rev?" grumbled a couple of men.

I released the ravenous bunch, preoccupied with an unprecedented Harkhomes question—could there possibly be a closet poet among this literarily challenged crew?

Focus Your Vision

As an English major at Cornell University, I'd encountered the literary luminaries of the Harlem Renaissance for the first time: Claude McKay, Countee Cullen, Zora Neale Hurston, Alain Locke, and my favorite, Langston Hughes. Thinking about how Langston Hughes's words had somehow resonated with Arthur, I dusted off one of my Africana Center anthologies from that era and brought it to Harkhomes.

One night I invited Arthur to join me in my office. He sat reluctantly, suspicious that I had something up my sleeve, which I usually did when a resident was summoned to my weather-beaten card table of a desk. His reticence reminded me of his last office visit, the day he arrived at Harkhomes. He didn't say much during the standard new-resident interview—just the basics of another sad story.

A union plumber, Arthur had been doing construction work in New York City for many years, but a serious injury on the job put him out of work for almost a year. When he was cleared to work again, he was less productive because of lingering pain, so he wasn't assigned as many jobs, and the financial pressure and personal frustration mounted, causing domestic strife. Despondent, he started drinking, and after a drunken quarrel turned violent, his wife left with the children. Arthur stopped working altogether, was evicted, and ended up homeless.

"So you know the poetry of Langston Hughes?"

He looked away nervously.

"I heard you recite the words." I insisted.

"Mom was an English teacher, made us kids memorize some of the stuff from her Harlem Renaissance heroes," he recollected.

"Did they inspire you like Mom?"

"Dad committed suicide, Mom got depressed, lost her job. The literary guys couldn't help pay the bills. You don't defer dreams that die."

I could understand, given his unfortunate history, how Arthur felt such cynicism and defeat, but I was, as ever, determined to break through, so I pressed on.

"I found this old college book," I said, handing him the Harlem Renaissance Reader. "I thought that you might—"

He pushed it away. "Sorry, Rev, some dreams die easy." He hurried off.

I stared at the dog-eared paperback for a long time. So much for poetry.

I couldn't stop thinking about Arthur's distinction between deferred and dead dreams, fearing that the Harkhomes men fell largely into the latter group. So during the next morning's fellowship, I stayed with the biblical Joseph as a role model, stressing the importance of possessing a big picture for their lives, exhorting them, "Dust the cobwebs off of your dreams. Imagine where you want to be in your life one year from now, two years from now, five years from now, ten years from now. Whatever the dream is, reach for it anew, cling to it, refuse to let it go. If the future focus is bright, it will bring light to today's pathway!"

Feeling a little bit of energy from my tough crowd, I pushed the envelope and assigned homework for the first time, challenging them to spend some time asking themselves some questions and writing down the answers:

What do I most enjoy doing?

When am I most confident?

At what activities am I most competent?

What activities/subjects do I like the best?

What are my special talents and capabilities?

What are my proudest achievements?

What about my life excites me the most right now?

What is my dream for my life?

Managing my expectations, I was prepared the next day for just a handful of responses. In fact, no one did homework—not one. When I threatened extra chores, excuses deluged me. I was incredibly frustrated. I had tried every approach—literary, biblical, practical, pedagogical, and preachy—yielding not an iota of inspiration. Or so I thought, until a surprising development.

Face Your Valley

Arthur's office visit a few days later was unsolicited. My mouth dropped open when he handed in the completed homework.

"You are full of surprises," I declared, perusing his assignment.

"Joseph had a rough time with his vision," he said, plopping down in a metal folding chair.

"So you've been reading Genesis?"

"Quite a story. He was sold into slavery, ended up in another country, and then was unjustly thrown in prison."

"Did you have a rough time with your vision, too?" This was obviously a rhetorical question. He knew that I knew. Today, finally, he cracked the door.

"I wanted to be a teacher, like Mom," he whispered haltingly, as if each word carried its own burden of pain.

He hesitated; it seemed like forever. *Should I ask the next question or just wait?* I wondered. I waited, and silently prayed for grace.

"After Dad died," he finally continued, "Mom stopped working, things got real tight. I quit school, started working. Uncle got me in as an apprentice, plumber's union. I hated the union work and guys, but I needed the money, so I was stuck there, hoping my break would come. But after I got injured, I gave up on my dreams."

He buried his head in his hands. Not knowing what to say, I put my hand on his shoulder and prayed.

The exchange with Arthur encouraged me to dig deeper into the biblical Joseph, his journey from slave—betrayed by members of his own family—to prison inmate—falsely accused of rape by his boss's wife. "Joseph's mountaintop of vision was followed by his valley of adversity," I said, connecting the dots for the residents in my morning sermonette. "Your valleys represent those high obstacles, when your problems seem to have gotten the best of you, when your burdens seem unbearable and barriers insurmountable. Who's in the valley right now?"

All hands shot up, including Arthur's, whose countenance was never brighter. I silently celebrated the unprecedented feat of striking a collective Harkhomes nerve. What a difference a day—and a topic—make!

Gus described being downsized out of his job. "That's a circumstantial valley," I explained.

"I was in the wrong place at the wrong time because of a wrong friend," Street reported. I categorized his experience as a social valley.

Two men touched on the last-hired-first-fired syndrome. "Racism is an institutional valley," I asserted.

When I recognized Arthur's raised hand, the room went quiet. "I'm afraid of the future," he said quietly.

I nodded my head sympathetically, knowing many others in the room felt the same way. "Personal valleys are those inner challenges—the doubts, the fears, the disappointment, the fatigue, the past failures—which can cause you to give up on your dreams. If your dreams are strong, they can help you overcome whatever obstacles lie before you, preparing for the expected adversity and opposition, battling them, not letting them knock you off track. Focus your vision so that you can face your valley."

The joy of having my usually detached audience fully engaged didn't last long. Rickey, who'd stepped out to the bathroom, rushed in. "Rev, you need to see this." I followed him outside to 129th Street, with several men, including Arthur, trailing. Rickey pointed at my car, a used Chevy that I'd recently purchased because the drug dealers on the block had vandalized my last car beyond repair. I stared in disbelief at my Chevy: every window smashed, every tire slashed—damaged worse than the last time.

Arthur put a consoling hand on my shoulder. I shrugged it off. I paced around my desecrated car, trying to contain my anger.

The 129th Street drug dealers had targeted me from the beginning. The week I opened Harkhomes, one of the drug dealers who frequented the block approached me and beckoned me off into the shadows to talk. Flashing a roll of bills, he told me he would make it worth my while if I would move the shelter off the block. He didn't have anything against me or the homeless, he explained—"It's just 'bidness.'"

The threat was now clear to me. Not only was I cleaning up the place, bringing new people around, initiating constructive energy, getting in the way of their activities; they also fingered me as a dangerous competitor to their business because I was stealing their "customers" by helping them get off drugs. Every man I cleaned up at Harkhomes was one less sale for them. The dealers wrote threatening messages in chalk on the sidewalk in front of the shelter, but I'd send a man to scrub it off right away.

Valleys had abounded throughout my work at Harkhomes: church trustees opposed to "a dangerous project"; fair-weather volunteers who failed to show up for duty; donors whose checks bounced, yielding an overdrawn account and unpaid bills; burdensome regulations that temporarily closed the shelter for a missing exit sign; not-in-my-back-yard neighbors complaining about "undesirables," and on and on.

These external obstacles were formidable, but nothing compared to my inner ones. The drug dealers brought out the worst of my fears. I ignored the men's pleas to get back inside, pushed Arthur out of the way, and stormed off.

Fuel Your Victory

Wearing a borrowed hoodie and sunglasses, I slipped into the block the next day, still stuck in the depths of my personal valley. Wavering between shutting down Harkhomes and operating incognito, I kept looking over my shoulder, preoccupied that the drug dealers' threats might be made real at any moment. As I walked swiftly up the street toward Harkhomes, I was relieved to see a handful of the men approaching me to usher me inside.

I knew from earlier experiences that reporting the threats and vandalism to the police precinct would fall on deaf ears and there would be little they could—or would—do to protect me and the shelter. To my surprise, Arthur recruited some fellow residents—a couple of Jesus Hunters joined in—to form a security force to safeguard my travels to and from Harkhomes. They called themselves Posse RJ (short for Rev. Joe).

A couple of posse members were former drug dealers, which worked to my advantage. One of them cannily negotiated a truce: the dealers agreed to leave me alone and in return we wouldn't cooperate with undercover investigations. Undercover operations? There hadn't been a police investigation on that block since the start of Harkhomes. It was like selling them snow in winter.

So the drug dealers and the shelter coexisted on West 129th Street for a while. I can't say that they respected me, but there were no more threats or vandalism. The turning point came when we transformed a large vacant lot that was being used for drug trafficking into a community garden. The dealers eventually moved their operations to another block, where they had less competition for customers.

By then I'd gone through two good pairs of shoes because I refused to invest in another car—even a junkyard-worthy used one. Posse RJ made the difference, not only helping me face my valley of fear and overcome it, but also keeping the doors of the shelter open and cleaning up the block.

My daily trips with Posse RJ gave me time to talk with Arthur. Up to this point, Arthur and initiative were contradictory terms. He would agree to see the physical therapist for his old work-related injury, then miss his appointment. He would be on his way to an AA meeting but would just keep going instead of attending. He was late for meals, and sometimes he didn't eat at all. Content with being completely idle, he would just sit around for as long as he could get away with it.

However, during one of our walks, Arthur talked again about the biblical Joseph and recounted the climax of that story. Despite the many obstacles he faced, Joseph never gave up on his vision and eventually attained his dreams of ascendance. His ability to interpret the king's dreams exalted him to a lofty status—governor of Egypt, second only to Pharaoh himself. Joseph was now in the leadership position he'd envisaged, with the power to save his country—and his family—from impending famine.

"So Joseph held on to his vision through the valley and got the victory," I summarized for him. "What about you?"

Arthur opened up about his family, how much he missed his wife and two daughters. "My wife and I have long dreamed," he mused, "about moving out of the Harlem walk-up to a our own home with a yard for the girls to play."

"When was the last time you saw them?" I asked.

He didn't answer and was quiet for the rest of the Posse RJ walk.

Back at Harkhomes, I researched Arthur's file and found his entry card; his emergency contact contained his wife's name and phone number.

My idea was to reconnect him with his family, and let him touch once again the victorious vision he had lost. Would she come? Would he be receptive? Would the visit inspire him? Should I take the risk?

His wife, Gail, was happy to hear from me and gladly agreed to visit with their two teenage girls. "I haven't heard from him forever," she worried. "Is he okay?"

"Seeing you and his girls will mean so much to him," I assured her. "Will you bring a recent family photo for your husband?"

"I'll take a new one for the occasion," she promised.

I decided to keep it a surprise, scheduling Posse RJ just to make sure Arthur was around at the appointed hour. When his family arrived, Arthur was shocked as well as ashamed that they had to see him in his current plight. But these negative feelings quickly passed, and the joy of being with his family again altered his mood. He smiled and joked and laughed for the first time since coming to Harkhomes.

The highlight of the visit was the photo that his family gave him. It was a beautiful framed portrait of his wife and daughters. Touched, he gave them a collective bear hug—more emotion than he'd ever shown; he was not the warm-and-fuzzy type. After they left, Arthur carried the photo around for the rest of the day, staring at it periodically for minutes at a time.

His family's visit brought about his turnaround. The sullenness faded, motivation resettled upon him, and the determination to change set in. Nothing could have worked better to renew Arthur's vision and refill the tank of his motivation than to see his wife and kids alive and well, right before his very eyes.

The family photo kept that vision alive. Arthur placed it on the floor beside his cot at night so his family was the last sight of the passing day and his first sight in the dawning one. When a fellow resident— on the way to the bathroom in the middle of the night—accidentally stepped on it and cracked the frame, Arthur immediately used what money he had and borrowed the rest to buy the best replacement frame he could afford for his most treasured possession.

The physical image became a mental picture of Arthur's dream—a reunited family in a new home—and this vision fueled his victory over all the practical, everyday steps to achieve it.

Arthur resolved to get a job, but finding employment was tough. Because of his injuries, he was no longer able to do construction work, so the job search became an arduous, time-consuming process. Arthur looked for weeks, eventually finding a job as a security guard, claiming that his leadership running Posse RJ prepped him for the opportunity.

Arthur prospered at his security job. When his company won a big new contract, he became a supervisor, and working as much overtime as possible, he ended up making nearly as much money as he had on the construction job. He moved out of Harkhomes and back in with his family. He worked a second job, earning extra money, saving up for that home with a backyard, keeping his dream alive.

Sharpen Your Tools

The *vision tool* is all about how you see your future. For it is human nature to dream, to envision victories won, to imagine better times, to hope for brighter days. Discouragement, difficulty, distraction, and doubt will tempt you to give up on your dreams. Follow these steps to maintain a positive view of your future and to stay motivated to bring your dreams to life.

Step one: Frame your glory plan. Meditate on what and where you want to be one year from now, five years from now, ten years from now. Envision the future picture for your life, in all its spectacular glory. The word *picture* can be used as both a noun and a verb—it's both something you *have*, and something you *do*. If you're like Arthur, a "picture" of success isn't a metaphor, it's literal—an actual photograph or page torn from a magazine or even a memorable saying or favorite poem. Or perhaps your glory plan is best articulated in words or bullet points that outline your goals and/or describe a detailed picture of your ideal future. Whatever the case—picture or words or both—it's important to have something tangible that you can hang on the wall or bulletin board and/or carry in your wallet or handbag. Pull out your vision at least once a day as a constant reminder of what it is you're aiming to achieve. It will drive you forward.

Step two: Figure out your valley. Face those forces that represent the greatest threats to you fulfilling your goals. Your valleys signify the rough road ahead: the disappointments and setbacks, the doubts and fears that stand between you and your dreams. Your valleys exist to test your vision, to see how real and strong it is. Don't let the adversities of life take you by surprise. Know that the obstacles are coming. Be prepared. Don't shrink back in the midst of a crisis. Instead, with a positive Tude, focus on figuring out the best strategy for enduring your valley, for rising out of it. Joseph of Scripture landed in prison before his rise to leadership. So did Nelson Mandela. Your plight may or may not be as hopeless as theirs. But, however deep your valley, climb out of it with your eye trained on the mountaintop of victory ahead.

Step three: Fuel your victory. Center each day on the inspiration of your vision. Live up to the standard of excellence that is inherent in your dreams. The key to daily victory is self-motivation—living with enthusiasm, purpose, conviction, vigor, and joy. Last year's dream or last month's purpose or last week's goal will not generate today's zest. Step outside of yourself to refresh your inner journey. Go to that special place where nature can uplift you: the power of the dawn, the beauty of the sunset, the glimmer of the full moon. Enter into that singular fellowship where inspiration flows. Share your dream with other dreamers and revel in the mutual affirmation, and your life will brim with motivation.

Step four: Fight for your dreams. Fight to hold on to your glory plan. Be a visionary warrior. Never lose sight of the big picture for your life in the details of responsibility or drudgery of obligation. Avoid *under-dreaming*—having a negative or limited view of your future, or no glory plan at all. It's better to start with a wrong or fuzzy picture that can be adjusted and clarified than with a blank screen. Err on the side of having too much vision rather than too little. Resist doubters and naysayers. If your relative or teacher or boss or peer says you can't do it, defend your dream. Prove them wrong. Be tenacious. Life passes quickly; the battle for your dreams happens now, not yesterday, not tomorrow.

Step five: Find the divine in your dreams. Look within—deep within—for your dreams. Joseph of Scripture dreamed of being the great one in his family. He ended up saving a nation. If you're having trouble discovering your dream, get to know your heart, the values that matter most, your deepest convictions and joys, and your vision will spring from there. And don't forget to dig spiritually—to pray, to ask God to reveal your divine destiny. Don't be in a hurry. Wait on divine revelation, which may manifest over time. Like the biblical dreamer Joseph thousands of years ago, God just might determine a greater purpose for you than what you have in mind for yourself.

YOUR VISION AFFIRMATION

I will see the big picture for my life, as glorious as the sky on a cloudless day, taking up a positive view of my future—motivated to overcome every obstacle in my way and soar beyond the storms on the wings of my dreams.

TOOL #3

SELF-ESTEEM
THE PASSION
BUILDING SELF-CONFIDENCE

Since the Harkhomes residents viewed my insistence on morning-and-evening Bible study as annoying overkill, I'd decided to substitute a little levity into one night's pre-meal reflection. "Who can tell me the playwright's favorite book of the Bible?"

I should have anticipated the blank stares. "The Acts of the Apostles."

The pervasive groans let me know that my joke bombed worse than expected.

"Hey, Rev, you know any dirty jokes?" Vibe queried, provoking a flurry of jeers at the absurdity of the notion. I quickly dug deep, hoping to discover a diamond to redeem myself.

"I know one about two lovers."

The disbelieving crowd egged me on.

"What was the secret of Delilah getting into Samson's house?"

The boos and hisses were simmering.

"She picked his locks."

The heckling erupted, signaling I'd created a crater. The pounding at the front door gave me an excuse for a getaway. Saved by the bell.

I opened the door for Tommie, a fiftysomething-year-old black man, who'd arrived seeking shelter with good timing: an empty Harkhomes bed was a rare occurrence, but we happened to have one. Yet he was so disheveled, so odorous, that I wondered if I should admit him. His pleading eyes persuaded me to rescue him. He also expressed gratitude, possessed a warm, engaging smile, and had a charming way of using big words, if in a slightly confused way.

I ordered the extreme-scrub protocol, an intensive cleanup procedure I initiated for long-term, subway-dwelling homeless men like Tommie. I assigned Vibe, the youngest and most energetic of the residents, to lead the team, which immediately went to work. They peeled the rancid clothes off Tommie's body; bagged and took them to the curbside garbage can; hurried him off to the shower with disinfectant soap and shampoo, with Homie hovering to enforce their use; meanwhile, others fetched clean clothes from the stash of donations. Tommie emerged from the makeover routine a new man.

He ravaged all the dinner leftovers, received his linens, and made his cot. He seemed to be settling in, but within an hour he was back in the office.

"I can't stay here," he uttered.

"Why not? What happened?" My probing questions went unanswered. I asked Tommie to wait while I quickly inquired among the residents why Tommie had been alienated so quickly. Everyone was just as perplexed as I was. I urged him to change his mind, and Vibe pleaded with him to stay, but Tommie pressed his way to the door. Finally, he broke down in tears, whispering: "I'm not good enough to stay here." With those words, he walked out the door. I never saw Tommie again.

Conceive of Yourself as Important

It was one of those endless nights at Harkhomes. I felt low over the loss of Tommie, so I wrote to distract myself from another defeat. While the men slumbered—and particularly on tough nights like this—it was often my habit to write myself to sleep, a kind of literary therapy as I purged the burdens of running Harkhomes by releasing them through pen to paper.

That late night I found no peace as I dashed off thoughts about the awful truth of Tommie's experience. When adversity strikes and circumstances turn for the worse, an individual's self-worth can follow this downward trend. Tommie had internalized the jagged realities of his troubled life, which made it impossible for him to see himself living in a place that would challenge his identity and change his destiny. When assistance was offered to him, he refused it; he let his fear of failure drive him away from an opportunity to leave his broken life behind. He did not accept help because he did not consider himself worthy of help.

In the futility of the moment, I let my imagination roam, scribbling out realities that defied resolution, except for a fictional minister, Leroy, who with Solomonic wisdom found a way. I became Minister Leroy; Harkhomes turned into the Lighthouse Shelter; eight motley men represented the real-life residents who were, in my creative musings, involved in a classic whodunit to be solved by Charlie, a fictional police officer loosely based on one of the TV cops from one of the prime-time crime shows that I hardly had time to watch. My notes and writings from that night evolved into the stage play *Homegrown*, which in addition to being (I hope) a satisfying and engrossing mystery was also inspirational, in that it showed an ensemble of broken men becoming whole again.

That night, Tommie became Professor, a character whose flawed personality reflected the breakdowns of the real person who had come in and out of my life so quickly just hours before. As I conceptualized Professor in the image of Tommie, I discovered that both real and imagined persons had a self-esteem problem.

I paced, struggling through a character description: "Diffidence— the still-hovering cloud of his troubled past—characterizes his behavior. His speech is affected with a misguided eloquence, firing words and phrases like a soldier fighting a guerilla war with bayonet tactics." . . . *No, not quite right. . . .*

As I stumbled over revisions, Vibe appeared. "Sleepwalking again?" he teased me. My nocturnal habits had become a source of good-natured ribbing

"Something like that. What about you? Why are you still up?" I inquired.

"Thinking about Tommie."

"Me too. I'm actually writing about him."

I described the play I was working on and the Tommie-inspired character.

He laughed. "Yo, man, I'm an actor. Can you write me into the script, too?"

We spent the next hour talking about his failed New York City acting career—a familiar story indeed. His plot twist was the way he internalized all the audition rejections he experienced. A music lover, he had tried to break in with some groups in the new hip-hop trend but got nowhere. He took it all personally, got depressed, lost his job waiting tables, was evicted, and became suicidal. An ex-girlfriend found him with a loaded pistol, wavering over pulling the trigger. Her brother referred him to Harkhomes, but he almost left after his first night because "everyone was treating me so nice."

"I know how Tommie feels," he revealed.

"We were unable to help Tommie because he could not conceive of himself as important," I said, and then seized the opportunity to inject a foundational biblical principle into the discussion.

"Remember my teaching about Moses?"

"Didn't he say something about not speaking well?" Vibe recalled, to my thinly veiled delight.

"He told God, 'I am not eloquent,' because he suffered from poor self-image, which held him back from obeying the divine call."

I offered him an Old Testament contrast: the prophet Isaiah, who, when faced with the option of accepting his divine commission, responded, "Here I am. Send me."

"The difference in their responses," I explained, "was due to different levels of their self-esteem. Isaiah's was high. Moses's was low."

"Like Tommie and me," he affirmed.

"You got it!" I overreacted, amazed that one of my scriptural seeds had found fertile soil at midnight. "Tommie missed his appointment with destiny tonight," I continued enthusiastically, "because the blinders of a negative self-image blocked his ability to accept the fact that we all—including you, especially you!—are important in God's eyes because you are created in His image and likeness. Conceiving of yourself as a child of the Ruler of Heaven and Earth will give you the confidence to overcome whatever obstacles you face in life."

Vibe sat there, pensive. I prayed for him, then he returned to his cot in the Fellowship Room. I stretched out on my cot in the hallway. Though not for very long, I slept pretty good that night.

Commit to Your Passion

Countless rewrites of *Homegrown* over the next few months lead to two staged readings at the National Black Theatre, a landmark Harlem theater that eventually staged a full production of the play. During rehearsals, the director, Dwight Cook insisted that the actors of *Homegrown* meet the men of Harkhomes.

Art met life around the Fellowship Room table one evening as the Harkhomes residents advised the visiting thespians about fictionalizing our 129th Street reality into a 125th Street loft-theater space.

Inspiration found Vibe that night as he bounced from actor to actor, plying them with questions, collecting tidbits of meaning for his own life. Afterward, he begged me to take him to a rehearsal. Though I made it seem like a tough decision, I was delighted to bring him into an environment where he would connect to professional actors with whom he might share common experiences and gain some self-confidence.

A long-term amateur actor performing bit roles in church plays, I'd approached Dwight about playing Minister Leroy, the reluctant hero of the drama, because I thought there'd be some sort of poetic justice in realizing in fiction what I was failing to do every day in real life. Instead, much to my chagrin, he cast me as Professor, the protagonist I'd modeled after forlorn Tommie.

The night Vibe came to rehearsal, the stage manager was out sick. My special guest happily stepped in, and his good work caught the eye of the gregarious producer, Tunde Samuel, who recruited Vibe as his own special assistant to help with lights, sound, costumes, curtains, coffee runs, and the like. Tunde saw the potential in the young man and mentored him in all aspects of theater operations.

Vibe became a regular at rehearsals, even subbing once—at Tunde's direction—for the absent actor playing Slice, whose character description was eerily similar to his own profile: "The youngest of the men, he is a subject of collective concern. Though it's against the rules, he slips on the Walkman whenever he can, grooving to the beat; the rap rhythm becomes him. His effusiveness and bravado shield the vulnerability of a boy forced to be a man before his time." Clearly I drew inspiration from Vibe in conceiving Slice, even if I didn't consciously set out to do so.

After weeks of relentless rehearsals—Vibe enjoyed them more than I, especially after he became the official understudy for Slice's role—it was finally opening night. As my fellow actors and I took up positions on the dark National Black Theatre stage on opening night, I pressed my hands tightly against my thighs to keep them from quivering. Since I'd written the opening scene to reenact wake-up time at Harkhomes, I was presently in the fictional stage set of the Fellowship Room, pretending to sleep on a portable cot.

Before the lights came up, I glanced stage right and saw Vibe, hands on the ropes, ready to open the curtains—his Tunde-appointed responsibility for opening night, an important assignment that highlighted the confidence his diligence at the rehearsals had earned.

Vibe had become so passionate about his commitment to *Homegrown* that he created a role for himself—my acting coach, offering advice (often gratuitously) on the tone, rhythm, volume, timing, and inflection of my dialogue. So when I flawlessly delivered my first line—"If my recollection ceases to fail me, I do indeed reminiscence the half fortnight ago when we were premissable for a most protracted slumbering"—I knew in my heart that part of the credit went to my unlikely mentor Vibe.

I was thrilled, if somewhat surprised, to witness the degree to which Vibe was uplifted by the return of his passion for acting and the theater.

When he first arrived at Harkhomes filled with despair and defeat, Vibe approached the Harkhomes regimen as drudgery, the flip side of passion—shades of gray instead of a rainbow. Life was one big obligation. Everything was difficult, painful, a chore. He lethargically and perfunctorily made one complaint after another. Bored and negative, he was just going through the motions of life.

Does this Vibe remind you of anyone? . . . Of yourself?

But when Vibe started volunteering at the National Black Theatre, each rehearsal became an adventure into the world of performing arts that he believed had passed him by. He rediscovered his love for theater and committed himself to it, spawning a strong and positive energy, a spirit of enthusiasm and dedication.

Vibe's experience strengthened my conviction about a direct, if hard-to-measure, correlation between the degree to which you're passionate about a task and your chances of succeeding at it. Let's face it: at the end of the day, nothing boosts self-confidence like success, which usually comes as the result of working hard at something; and you work hardest at the things that you love.

You can certainly achieve some things without being passionate about them. You can even accomplish some tasks perfectly well despite the fact that you actively dislike doing them—you grit your teeth and simply grin and bear it.

Vibe is not one of those people. Neither am I one of those people—most of us aren't. The difference between Vibe and me was that I discovered my passion for writing early, as a preteen, when my essay—"Key Moments in Negro History"—won a grade school competition. I had never before won anything in my life. I felt so good about myself that I kept writing.

In college I became an English major, and my love of literature rather than political science, biology, or sociology propelled me to the dean's list every semester. Mired in the drudgery of law school studies, creative writing—purely for recreation—was my release. But passion can take on a life of its own, bringing you to new extraordinary experiences and the realizations of goals and dreams. This was my case when a college paper about the great nineteenth-century African American leader Booker T. Washington became an Off-Broadway play, *Cast Me Down*, and when my sleepless-night scribbling about the homeless grew into the well-received production of *Homegrown*.

When Vibe reconnected to his passion and the joy that came with it, he began to think and feel differently about himself, as someone who was valuable to someone else, someone who kept his word, someone who could control himself, and most important of all, someone who could be trusted. He felt too good about himself and the progress he was making to let anything derail his newly inspired life. This outcome is what's most important about finding and committing to your passion: doing so leads not just to outward success, but to genuine, inner satisfaction, peace, and real fulfillment. That, in the end, is what the inspired life is all about.

Several months later, Vibe and I sat in the Harkhomes office, talking about the ongoing challenges of shelter life. He'd moved out a few weeks ago into his own room, sustained by a stage-managing job at a downtown theater, to which he'd been referred by Tunde. When he visited tonight as the guest in the mentor speaking series that I'd launched—his first time back at Harkhomes since he'd left—he was greeted like a conquering hero, which made him feel really good about himself.

I told him about Larry, a new resident, the youngest man, so down on himself that he always talked about leaving Harkhomes. "Sound familiar?"

"Been there, done that," Vibe affirmed, then with conviction, added, "I got him."

As we entered the Fellowship Room for dinner, Vibe was a man on a mission. As the guest speaker, he needed no introduction. As we ate, he regaled us with stories from the National Black Theatre "internship" and his new job. Riotous laughter broke out when he recounted how I left out one of my lines on opening night. He could've left that part out.

He even entertained us with a monologue from Slice, the *Homegrown* character he understudied. Adding his own creative choreography as he bounced around the Fellowship Room, Vibe riveted us with his rendition of the song his character performed in *Homegrown*, the "Glory Rap."

> *I was*
> *Up and down*
> *Ain' no clown*
> *But circumstances*
> *Took my chances*
> *Druggin'*
> *Drinkin'*
> *Drivin'*
> *Da women crazy*
> *Ain' no maybe*
> *I was da king*
> *Dey loved my sting*
> *I ran an' lusted*
> *'Til I got busted*

All were now on their feet, grooving with Vibe's beat. It was the first time a guest speaker—any speaker—brought the crowd to a stand.

Even with the infinitude of my sermonizing, I'd never come close to slowing down their forks.

It was all a hustle

In prison

No reason

I was lost in bustle

Bluff

Fluff

Shake

Fake

Same ol' story

It's so gory

Same ol' news

Da Harlem blues

'Til I stumble

On the Bible

Made me humble

Was caught

I fought

But found surrender

It was so tender

Soft and sweet

It was the peace

Way down in-

Side, I felt it

Confessed my sin

An' I melted

Mystery
I touched it
Eternity
I reached it
Not knowin'
Still goin'
Faith was my call
Now I got it all

As he sang, Vibe moved around the room and was now face-to-face with Larry, grooving a connection to him—building his self-confidence with every beat.

God does it best
I am so blessed
With grace, peace, and love
From up above
Jesus my groove
Greatest move
Ever made
No more fade-
Ing out
Want to shout
Got it made now
Glory is the news
I beat the blues now
Glory all the way
A brighter day now

The men clapped and cheered. Larry was the first one to give Vibe a high-five. Connection affirmed!

Afterward, with the meal over and his table cleared, Vibe's tone turned serious. "The moment in *Homegrown* that really touched me was when Sarge says to Rocky: 'I cried because I had no shoes, until I saw the man who had no feet.'

"When I heard that line, I realized that I'd been feeling sorry for myself," he confessed, "wallowing in self-pity. I remembered the time this guy Tommie came here but left. As bad as my situation was, his was so much worse. I decided to spend time helping guys like Tommie, to take my mind off my own problems."

He reached in his pocket, pulling out some notes. "When I looked inside myself, searched my heart for those things that mean the most to me, I found my passion again. I took notes from Rev's talks and my mentor Tunde at the theater, so here are some questions you to need to ask yourselves to discover your passions.

"What do I most enjoy doing? Why? What are the things in my life that bring me the most meaning? Why? What are my gifts? How do I best express them?"

I was taking notes, capturing these gems for future distribution. I glanced over at Larry. I was thrilled to see that he, too, was taking notes!

Vibe continued, "What activities make me full of energy? What are my greatest thrills in life? When do I most often experience them? What are the things that I would keep doing for the rest of my life even if I wasn't getting paid for it?"

Vibe then facilitated a discussion about the inner journey to passion, fielding answers to his questions. It was so amazing to me to see how quickly the pupil had surpassed his teacher. I had already decided I would beg him to return to speak at dinner next week. And then he got deeper still.

"Don't be disappointed if you're unable to answer all of the questions, or if you're struggling to come up with a single answer," Vibe encouraged his rapt audience. "Lifting your self-esteem is a process; it's taken me a long while. But it starts with your inner journey; it brings you in closer touch with those sometimes hidden, hard-to-get-at thoughts and feelings about your values, about what matters most."

I knew in that moment that he'd learned to use a tool of self-esteem, and by teaching others about it, he was demonstrating just how high his self-confidence had gone.

Sharpen Your Tools

The *self-esteem tool* is all about how you see yourself. You can't value your life and be deserving of your dreams if you don't value yourself and believe that you're worthy of success. Don't internalize the difficult realities of life that can bring down your self-worth, or fall prey to letting others opinions dictate how you see yourself. Instead, follow these steps to help you think in a different way—a positive way, an inspirational way—about yourself and your ability to handle whatever challenges lie before you.

Step one: Know your glory. You are made in the image of God and in His likeness; thus you are created great by God. "You have made them a little lower than the angels and crowned them with glory and honor" (Psalm 8:5). You possess inherent worth and are set in the natural environment with personal responsibility and real freedom. You don't need people's approval; you have God's. You are not limited by who your father or mother was or was not; what neighborhood you grew up in; what schools you attended; or which race or class you were born into. You are not defined by the size of your house, the status of your job, or the state of your marriage. You have limitless potential in God's eyes. Strive to see yourself from God's boundless point of view, not from society's narrow standards.

Step two: Know your wholeness. As noted above, you are divinely created—made a composite of spirit, soul, and body. It is human nature to be body conscious; it is the most visible part of you, which you feed and clothe, exercise and pamper. Your body can affect your self-image. For example, if you're overweight, sick, or injured, you can feel bad about yourself. Your soul is the seat of your emotions, which can also influence self-esteem. If you fail at marriage, school, work, or anything else and feel bad about it, like Tommie, your self-esteem can plummet. Your spirit connects with God's spirit, the ultimate source of high self-worth. Moses came to understand who he was because of God's grace, which gave him the confidence to fulfill his calling and bring free-dom and justice to his people. Make sure you're in touch with all three parts of you, but cultivate your spirit—your most important dimen-sion. Grow spiritually and you will not only feel great about yourself, but you will radiate your inner life.

Step three: Find your passion. Find something you're passionate about and do it. Nothing will lift your self-esteem more than taking on a task you're passionate about, applying yourself, using your gifts, sticking with it, building on your abilities, and seeing the enterprise through to successful completion. Whether it's playing the saxophone or mowing lawns or taking pictures or writing novels or sweeping floors or running a business or preaching a sermon, if you do it with passion and commitment, you'll not only achieve excellence, but you'll find fulfillment in it. You'll never be truly happy doing something that oth-ers want *for* you but that you don't really want for yourself. You've got to be practical, but you've also got to be true to yourself if you want to succeed. Now is the time to discover what excites and drives you, which will help you feel good about yourself and your contributions to the world. Identify your unique gift and cultivate it. Resurrect a talent and develop it. Unbury a skill and take it to a higher level. Build self-confi-dence into your life by thriving with the things you love to do.

Step four: Flourish with your passions. Life is very busy and there are only so many hours in a day, but you owe it to yourself to find the time and space to dedicate to your passions—you deserve it. If your passion is not consistent with your livelihood, moonlight. Don't quit your day job, but find a way to cultivate your passion in your spare or leisure time. One way to think about this: work practically by day; work passionately by night. Never neglect your responsibilities, but don't let them crowd out your passions. As you follow your passions, you will unearth the elements out of which greatness, excellence, splendor, and genius are made. Let new inspiration rise from being passionate about what you do, by working hardest at the things you love. As you live life as an adventure in pursuit of your passions, you will value and affirm yourself.

Step five: Do good, feel good. It can be easy to fall into the trap of self-pity ("Nothing ever goes my way"), which leads to self-loathing, both of which are highly toxic emotions to be avoided at all costs. Instead, channel the energy you use in feeling sorry for yourself into showing compassion for others. Realize the truth of the statement "I cried because I had no shoes, until I saw the man who had no feet," which reminds us that there are always folks in more dire straits. Which is not to encourage you to seek comfort in another's misery, but to inspire you to have perspective on whatever you believe to be your challenges by considering there is always someone worse off, like the millions of refugees in war-ravaged societies. So when you feel the urge to throw a pity party, cancel it and reach out to someone who needs help. It will take your mind off your own problems and foster a sense of moral accomplishment, making you feel more useful and purposeful, lifting your self-image to new heights.

SELF-ESTEEM AFFIRMATION

I will accept and affirm myself, just as I am, just the way God made me, refusing to let past and present problems, the haters and the naysayers define me; committing to my passions; using my gifts anew; devoting myself to excellence; and feeling great about myself.

TOOL #4

DISCIPLINE
THE POEM
BUILDING PERSEVERANCE

Standing in the tiny Harkhomes kitchen—it was not even a room but just a wall in the basement back hallway—I listened to Sandi take issue with the morning topic as he washed dishes.

"What?!...Pain?!...You kidding, right, Rev?" Sandi challenged me.

"It's short-term pain," I tried to encourage him. "Short-term pain for long-term gain." I summarized the metaphorical process for discipline, the principle of self-denial, the regimen of personal sacrifice, the process of giving things up in order to get ahead. "Discipline is the frontline in the battle for your personal progress."

"I ain' sign up for pain," he insisted.

The negative reaction of Sandi, among others—he was just the loudest—to my biblical theme of the day didn't break my stride. To illustrate it, I'd hit them with a paraphrase of Jesus from Matthew 16:24—"You must deny yourself, take up your cross, and follow me." To reinforce the point, I'd bludgeoned them with the Apostle Paul: "No discipline seems pleasant at the time, but painful. Later on, however, it produces a harvest of righteousness and peace for those who have been trained by it" (Hebrews 12:11).

I'd been talking about this tool for a while but hadn't yet found a palatable way to articulate it. I tried to soften the blows. "I'm not really in favor of pain—only pain for a purpose. It's about sacrificing something for now, tolerating something unpleasant, maybe even suffering a little bit, for the sake of making strides forward, of achieving something bigger. So pain is not suffering for suffering's sake, but suffering for the sake of getting from here to there."

By the perfect silence, blank looks, and Sandi's rebuttal, it was becoming increasingly clear that pain as a life skill was the least popular of the touchstones in my growing toolbox.

"Discipline . . . self-denial . . . perseverance . . . giving things up in order to get ahead. This is tough stuff, but once you realize this, and accept it, you will be better prepared psychologically for the personal sacrifices that are part and parcel of your pathway to success."

Silence.

I tried a familiar example. "It's like eating spinach growing up. You didn't like it, but it was good for you. And then you developed a taste for it."

"You got the wrong green, Rev." Sandi seized the moment. "We eat collards 'round Harlem."

Chuckles erupted all around.

My daily blooper—a fretful reminder of my interloping status—came at a really bad time. I was already struggling with whether to conclude the day's teaching with still some hope of redeeming the topic at a later time but fell prey to my irrepressible flaw of not knowing when to stop.

"Have you ever seen a baby chick try to peck its way out of an egg as it's hatching? The sight is agonizing to watch because it happens so slowly and the chick has to struggle so hard, pecking away tiny fragments of the eggshell, one little piece at a time. You may think nothing in the universe should have to endure that kind of struggle. You may think, 'Something must be wrong—surely nature didn't intend it to be this way.'"

Sandi stood up and started toward the door. My stare arrested him, reinforcing the punishment of extra chores that awaited anyone who walked out on my sermonettes. He sat back down. I quickly pressed on, sensing the ticking bomb.

"It's tempting to help the baby chick break out of that egg—to break the shell for him, to assist him in this seemingly impossible task. But guess what happens if you do that? *The chick dies.* It turns out that the struggle to peck its way out of the egg is what physiologically activates the resources the chick needs to live. Making his path 'easier' denies him the struggle nature intended him to have. It's the struggle *itself* that guarantees his life."

Without looking in my direction this time, Sandi walked out. I raised my voice to vanquish the "ohhs" and "ahhs" rising from his peers in his wake.

"Think of this little-known fact of nature whenever you're struggling to get out of your own 'eggshell' and feeling frustrated in the process. Remember, the chick's struggle to break free generates the vitality for life once free. The eggshell as the barrier of life becomes the essential source of life."

I was glad to hear a couple of affirming "amens"—my spiritual lingo was rubbing off a little bit—which bolstered me for the challenges waiting just outside the door.

Endure Your Short-Term Pain

As I discreetly watched Sandi scrub down the antiquated stove—the first in a weeklong series of chores as punishment for walking out of this morning's meeting—I reflected on his plight. Sandi's homelessness was the result of a complex set of problems, but at the root he was plagued by a frustrating lack of personal drive and discipline. He was lazy, gave up too easily, and shrank back from challenges, habitually waving the white flag of surrender at the first sign of crisis. Recently, he'd stopped going to his GED prep class yet again.

Sandi's story shared many of the hallmarks of tales of other homeless men Harkhomes served: he was born to a single mom on welfare; dropped out of high school; never knew his father; never had a 9-to-5 job; never had a place of his own. At Harkhomes, his life experience and undisciplined lifestyle were the rule, not the exception.

The roots of these men's problems ran deep. Their grandparents—sharecroppers who were the descendants of slaves—had fled to the promised land of the Harlem Renaissance. Instead of the Roarin' Twenties, these men and women were confronted with the Great Depression. Instead of the chains, whips, and nooses that had oppressed their forebears, they found substandard housing, poor education, inadequate health care, last-hired-first-fired employment, and glass ceilings everywhere—Jim Crow in a bow tie.

Sandi and his peers were the unfortunate heirs of this legacy of hardship, and the resulting pathologies represented a profound paradox. Though offspring of the fateful forces that had disadvantaged so many African Americans, they were still human souls whose God-given dignity demanded that they act with responsibility, vitality, and hope. I knew there were no easy answers, but my faith and a handful of victories encouraged me that there might be something in the toolbox that would work for Sandi.

Distracted by my contemplations, I missed making a timely inspection of Sandi's half-finished work on the stove—he was a master of going through the motions. I looked around for him but it was no surprise that he'd disappeared since today was a "check day," when every two weeks welfare checks arrived. These days were always something of a headache at Harkhomes. The men, newly flush with cash, had a tendency to give in to their worst impulses and vices. My efforts to balance material provision with spiritual resources and character development were rendered ineffectual.

"Hope deferred makes the heart sick, but a longing fulfilled is a tree of life" (Proverbs 13:12). I explored this Old Testament verse with the men that evening, reminding them—and me—not to give up hope.

The next day, I shared from the New Testament: "Consider it pure joy, my brothers and sisters, whenever you face trials of many kinds, because you know the testing of your faith produces perseverance. Let perseverance finish its work so that you may be mature and complete, not lacking anything" (James 1:2–4). "Try to find joy in your pain," I punctuated the passage.

Sandi gave me one of those "You got to be kidding, Rev" looks but didn't say a word and remained seated, not wanting to add to his punishment workload. "The fact you were raised in a broken family or went to a bad school, that's still no excuse for failure," I asserted, glancing at him. "It simply means working harder, being better. Racism—past or present—may hurt you in some way, but you got to get through it. It's just another barrier you've got to hurdle, another mountain to climb."

On the last day of his extra work detail, Sandi was mopping the bathroom floor, working as lethargically as ever. "Winston Churchill once made a statement you should think about." Why not try a historical example? Nothing else had worked.

"Winston who? Was he the guy who beat Hitler?"

"Exactly," I affirmed, deciding that it was best to keep it simple and embrace the little victory of getting his attention. "Churchill once made the statement, 'Never, ever, ever, give up.'"

"What ya sayin', Rev?" He stopped mopping, a tinge of angst in his voice.

Was the door of understanding finally opening? "There are times in life when you feel like giving up—fact of life. It happens to everybody. No one has a smooth and easy road to success."

"I ain' had no road, just lots of rocks."

His response called to mind Emerson whom I quoted. "Do not go where the path may lead, go instead where there is no path and leave a trail." I hesitated. If a twentieth-century statesman barely clicked, a nineteenth-century poet was too much of a stretch.

"Your rocks are adversity, disappointment, mistakes, defeat," I elaborated. "Perseverance is the will to keep on going when things are so bad that you feel like giving up."

"What's your pain, Rev?" he countered. "You had it easy. You ain' never had pain."

There was a universe of painful experiences that I could have shared with him: financial, social, emotional, and physical—which was the one I felt the most in that moment, the burnout caused by the countless nights sleeping in the shelter instead of home in my own bed.

But I concluded it would have been counterproductive to vent with Sandi. Instead, another Scripture came to me: "Carry each other's burdens, and in this way you will fulfill the law of Christ." (Galatians 6:2).

I met his eyes across the table and said, "My pain is your pain. I hurt because you hurt. I'm suffering because you and the other brothers are my burden to bear. So I have to keep on walking and not let the pain trip me up."

"Maya."

I'd stayed away from poems at Harkhomes since my Harlem Renaissance misadventures with Arthur. That Sandi recognized my last phrase from Maya Angelou seemed providential. Could poetry as a tool actually be making a comeback?

"You know Maya Angelou?"

"Ma's homegirl!" he exclaimed. "They both from St. Louie. Ma used to read her stuff aloud. That one I remember."

In moments like this I felt a divine grace and favor—I couldn't have imagined a more powerful connection. "Maya's message is especially for you. Don't wave the white flag of surrender at the first sign of trouble. Don't throw your hands up in frustration at your challenges. Don't give up. If you learn to walk with your pain, it will eventually go away."

Sandi put down the mop, folded his arms, leaned back against the counter, and looked up at the ceiling. I wasn't sure what, but something was happening. His question was a godsend.

"What's it mean, to keep walking with the pain?"

"Take the GED test again. Pass it this time."

"I don't like to study."

"That's the pain you got to walk."

"Can't make it."

"It's short-term pain."

I extended my hand. His arms remained folded. I pulled my hand back and prayed. "Lord, help Sandi to keep walking with the pain. Let him know that your yoke is easy and your burden is light."

I extended my hand again. I kept it there for what seemed like an eternity. He grudgingly shook it. I sensed this was the beginning of his change but I knew it wasn't going to be easy.

Embrace Your Long-Term Gain

Sandi started going again to the GED prep course. He got discouraged the first week and dropped out, the same old pattern of behavior.

"You forgot about homegirl Maya?" I challenged him.

"Just words—not helping me."

"You remember Naaman?" I asked, referring to the Old Testament military leader who was the subject of a recent morning fellowship.

"The general who was sick," he recalled.

"He had leprosy."

"I ain't sick."

"But like Naaman, you want a quick fix to your problem. He wanted a miraculous touch from the prophet Elisha to heal his disease. You want to show up to a prep class a couple of times and think the GED is done. Discipline doesn't work that way. Naaman wanted his healing badly enough that he dipped himself in the river seven times. Suffering for suffering's sake doesn't work. You get through the short-term pain by embracing the long-term gain."

Sandi then shared with me his goal of having his own place to live. I made the connection for him between the vision tool that had helped Arthur and the discipline tool that Sandi so direly needed. "Personal sacrifice must be linked to personal vision," I told him.

Sandi did return to GED class, struggling through it, failing the first test, ready to quit. "Naaman had to dip himself in the river seven times. You're just getting started," I said to him when he got his results.

He stuck with it this time—"walking with the pain," he affirmed—showing modest improvement on the next test. Then an unexpected blessing appeared: a Harkhomes volunteer who used to teach GED prep offered to be Sandi's private tutor. The third time around, Sandi passed.

When I acknowledged his triumph during dinner fellowship, Sandi, beaming, not only compared himself to Naaman but also encouraged his peers with the line from Maya Angelou's poetry.

As might be expected with someone who had never held a job of any kind, Sandi had trouble finding one. Of course, his criminal record didn't help either. After his first couple of interviews at fast food restaurants yielded rejections, I confronted his dejection with the reminder to embrace his long-term gain: "You need a job to get the rent for your own place." He grimaced, complained, acted out, and got angry—but he persevered.

Several interviews later, he reported he was a strong prospect for a porter job at a Harlem apartment building. But when the employer checked his address and discovered he was homeless, no job was offered.

Sandi was devastated. He'd had enough disappointment. I'd tried to encourage him with Churchill, Maya, Naaman, and other inspirational messages, to no avail. He headed for the door. I blocked his path, searching my mental file for scripture that might save the day, afraid of the adversity that awaited him outside.

"Got to go, Rev."

Then it hit me. "Let me give you something before you go."

I reached for my wallet and pulled out a dog-eared sheet of paper. I extended it to him, but he refused to take it. I'd hesitated to offer it before now because its author—Edgar Albert Guest, the "people's poet"—would be even more inscrutable to him than Churchill and lacked the cultural resonance of Maya. But it was the last resort.

"You asked me before about my pain. My most painful experience as a young man came as a football player in college."

"You played football, Rev?" Clearly he was surprised that a Bible-quoting, poetry-reciting nerd like me was once a jock.

"Did you play football?" I hoped for a connection.

"Running back. Loved it. But then I dropped out of school. It was over."

"I loved it, too, and was a running back, too. Got a college scholarship."

"Must've been pretty good."

"But the pain came. Football politics and injuries had me on the sidelines. It was the low point in my life. I was so discouraged I decided to quit football."

"You were really gonna give it up?"

"Yes, I really was. Too much disappointment and pain. I'd had enough. But my mom gave me this poem, the one I'm giving you. I read it. I didn't quit. I decided to walk with the pain and got to the long-term gain—becoming a record-setting, All-Ivy, All-American running back."

I extended the poem to him again. This time he took the paper and left. As I watched him walk down the street, I hoped that he'd read the words of the poem that had once inspired me over the rocky roads of my life.

> *You Mustn't Quit*
> *When things go wrong, as they sometimes will,*
> *When the road you're trudging seems all uphill,*

When the funds are low and the debts are high,
And you want to smile, but you have to sigh,
When care is pressing you down a bit,
Rest! if you must—but never quit.

Life is queer, with its twists and turns,
As every one of us sometimes learns,
And many a failure turns about
When he might have won if he'd stuck it out;
Stick to your task, though the pace seems slow—
You may succeed with one more blow.

Success is failure turned inside out—
The silver tint of the clouds of doubt—
And you never can tell how close you are,
It may be near when it seems afar;
So stick to the fight when you're hardest hit—
It's when things seem worst that YOU MUSTN'T QUIT.

I also prayed that Sandi would keep the poem and not deposit one of my most cherished mementos into the corner garbage can.

Sandi later told me that he started reading the poem after turning onto Lenox Avenue, past the garbage can. As he walked he read it again. He went to the park, sat down, and read it again. And again. And again. Sandi read it so many times that he began to memorize it.

He returned to Harkhomes that evening well before curfew.

The next day a friend of a friend called with news of a job opening as a dishwasher at a nearby restaurant. Sandi went in for the interview and got the job.

A few days later, I heard Sandi encouraging Con, one of the hard-core Henrys of Harlem, with these words: "Stick to the fight when you're hardest hit. It's when things seem worst that you mustn't quit!"

Amen, Sandi. Amen.

Sharpen Your Tools

American culture celebrates instant consumption and entitlement ("This is what I want it. Why can't I have it? *Now!*") as our highest values, glossing over the need for personal sacrifice. Mass media reinforces the tendency of human nature to take the easy road, to follow the path of least resistance, relegating the notion of painful endeavor to the rugged individuals of the frontier deep in America's past. The *discipline tool* runs counter to this cultural trend because it entails a two-step process. There's the decision to endure personal sacrifice *and* the commitment to maintain the *perseverance to follow through*. You have to get through the short-term pain to attain the long-term gain. Pain is reality. Failures and setbacks are inevitable. You may not like it but you have to manage it. The following steps will equip you with the tools to keep on going when your will falters, when the obstacles mount and when it feels like there's a hard wind blowing against you.

Step one: Be persistent. The journey of life is not a sprint but a marathon that requires you to persevere through detours, roadblocks, pitfalls, mudslides, and mountain climbs along the way. At some point, the adverse conditions will make you feel like giving up. Don't do it. Don't give up. You say—easier said than done. I say—to persist is a spiritual endeavor, a matter of your will, strength found in your inner life. When your body is overwhelmed with fatigue, when your soul is overcome with fear and doubt, it is your spirit that empowers you to stay the course. Determine in your heart that you will never, ever give up. Persistence is a choice: you choose—to give up or go on. Which will it be?

Step two: Be prepared. Expect things to sometimes go wrong. Life has an annoying way of upending your best-laid plans—no fault of your own. Everyday trials can cause events to spiral out of your control: tragedies, emergencies, calamities, problems, and chaos reign. Acknowledging that life could veer off track while you're pursuing your goals doesn't mean that the goals are wrong. And it doesn't mean that you should give up on those goals. It's all about your perspective—accept that something could go awry with your primary plan, so prepare a contingency plan. If plan A fails, be ready to move to plan B, C, or D. I'm not preaching pessimism but a realistic perspective on how unanticipated obstacles can pop up to deter your personal progress. Prepare for them; nip disappointment in the bud; move on to the next best thing.

Step three: Be patient. Expect outcomes to take longer than you would like. Waiting can be painful. People want what they want (or what they think they want) when they want it, which is invariably right now. Yet progress and inspiration usually take longer to happen than you think. So take your time; you will worry less and make fewer mistakes. Also, take the long view when estimating the time you need to achieve your goals: you will have more chances to take advantage of opportunities that you would have missed by speeding by. Finally, take a spiritual approach—"*Wait on the Lord: be of good courage, and He shall strengthen thine heart: wait, I say, on the Lord*" (Psalm 27:14, King James Version)—and you will release energy to welcome something amazingly divine to happen.

Step four: Be prudent. Expect life to be difficult. You will have to give things up to get ahead. Beware of immediate gratification—a root of potential trouble sowing seeds of excess into your life. Moderation in all things is the lifestyle rule you should apply and practice with diligence. Avoid behavioral extremes of all kinds: excessive desire for money (greed); excessive anger (violence); excessive appetite for sex (lust); excessive stress (a nervous breakdown); excessive desire for drugs or alcohol (addiction); excessive desire for food (gluttony); excessive affection (jealousy); or even an excessive competitive spirit (pride); this list goes on and on. The truth of the matter is that too much of anything, even if it begins as a good thing, can lead to stormy times. Be prudent and disciplined. Control your impulses and drives. To stop doing something that "feels good" may be the hardest thing you'll ever face. The sooner you learn to make the sacrifice, the better.

Step five: Be plucky. Expect to sometimes be assailed. That can be really painful. You may have the most wonderful personality in the world, but not everyone with whom you cross paths will like you. It's one of those unfortunate facts of life that someone will come along to mess up your plans, not necessarily because you did something to warrant adversaries, but because envy, jealousy, pride, mean-spiritedness, and ill will are human forces that we all have to deal with at one point or another. This is especially true if you're a leader or aspire to be one. Don't get bent out of shape when these saboteurs appear. Don't let them disrupt your plans. Adjust your expectations. You will have friends. You may have enemies. So see the opposition coming. Be ready for the haters. Expect them at inopportune times and from unknown places. If they don't come, so much the better. If they do, be courageous. Stare them down. Turn the other cheek. Overcome evil with good.

DISCIPLINE AFFIRMATION

I will concentrate on my long-term gain to get me through my short-term pain, determined to give something up in order to get ahead, willing to pay the price of personal progress, no matter the cost!

TOOL #5

ASSOCIATION
THE FELLOWSHIP
BUILDING CONSTRUCTIVE RELATIONSHIPS

I rushed into the small sanctuary of Bethlehem Pentecostal Assembly just upstairs from Harkhomes's basement shelter, upset that I was late because being even a second behind schedule with this group makes my tardiness—no matter how rare—a ready excuse for a resident's future lapse ("'Member the time you were late, Rev?!"). My anxiety quickly faded as I confronted the almost empty sanctuary before me.

After a year or so of meeting around the table in the Fellowship Room, I'd moved morning sessions upstairs once a week, hoping that coming up a flight of steps and sitting on a wooden pew in God's house might stir the men enough to keep more of them more alert and awake through my sermonette.

I'd been away for about a week, speaking to a church group in Vermont about inner-city ministry—and squeezed in a mini-vacation. Given the track record of slippage during my infrequent sojourns, this morning's sparse attendance was no surprise.

It was like herding cats, but I finally gathered the men in the sanctuary for a message that I'd spent most of my trip home from Vermont preparing. I'd been losing so many of them to bad relationship decisions that I decided to dig for a tool that might help them avoid destructive social choices.

Because I was a former athlete and continued to be a sports enthusiast, I'd previously approached this issue in terms of "teams." I'd thought this would be an easy metaphor for them: life is all about choosing sides, handpicking people you think will be best at helping your side win, teaming up with those who believe in you and your goals. Who's on your team, whether in sports or in life, can be the difference between winning the game or losing it, achieving your goals or falling short, living inspired or defeated. But I'd given up talking about teamwork because it hadn't worked for some reason; since that approach didn't get much traction, I was ready to try another.

I decided to break the ice with a joke. The humorous approach was always risky given my tough crowd and dismal track record, but I'd heard this one on my trip; it worked so well there . . . If it didn't work here, I'd blame it on New England frostiness.

"Did you hear about the missionaries who visited a tribe of cannibals?" I asked the group after opening prayer. Then waited a beat to build up to the punch line. "They wanted to give them a taste of religion."

Zee was the only one who chuckled. Karim shook his head in exasperation. "Rev, you gotta go gritty with your jokes. Like this one. Did you—"

"No profanity or X-rated humor allowed," I interrupted him.

"I got it. Did you hear about Zee's momma?" Karim offered.

"What about Zee's momma?" I played along. What was I thinking?

"Zee's momma so ugly, when she looks into the mirror, the reflection ducks."

Zee responded to Karim: "Yo momma so fat that all the restaurants in town have a sign that says: 'Maximum Occupancy—240 Persons or Yo Momma.'"

Karim retorted: "Yo momma so dumb that when you blew in her ear, she said, 'Thanks for the refill!'"

Zee fired back: "Yo momma so stupid that when I saw her yelling into an envelope and asked what she was doing, she said, 'Leaving a voicemail.'"

"Okay, okay, enough guys!" I said, raising my voice over the riotous laughter. I'd tried my best to join in their fun but was upset that my own ill-fated sense of humor had opened up the floodgates, which highlighted the counter-productivity of my ice-breaking stratagem; I decided to eschew going forward. Then I had second thoughts: as I looked around, my amused students were not only wide awake but fully engaged.

Flee Your Menace

It took a few minutes for things to settle down. I felt like I was launching the lesson into a rising tide. "Anybody know about the Old Testament figure Ahab?" I asked.

"Wasn't he the bad king?" answered Tuff, the only one who was following my advice to read the Bible daily.

"Ahab was really bad, doing more evil than any other king of his era. Micaiah the prophet refused to prophesy about Ahab. He didn't even want to go anywhere near him. The Ahabs of life are the trouble-makers to be completely avoided."

"Tuck had an Ahab," added Karim.

"Randy," several men affirmed.

A recovering drug addict who'd achieved the milestone of thirty days "clean," Tuck was a Harkhomes star: doing more than his share with chores and kitchen duty, even covering for others who'd fallen short. Randy, his main "get high" buddy, was coming regularly to visit Tuck but was not allowed to see him. "Whatever you do, stay away from Randy," I advised him. Tuck complied, understanding that Randy presented too great a temptation for him to forfeit his new, sober lifestyle and return to his old ways.

"Randy finally got to him," Steve, the only white resident at Hark-homes at that time, chipped in.

"What?" I exclaimed, scanning the room, finally realizing that Tuck wasn't there and the reasons for it.

"My bad," Chance confessed. "Randy slipped me a five and I gave Tuck the note."

"What note?" I asked, now eager to get the backstory to Tuck's downfall since it happened during my recent trip. I stifled my sigh. If only Harkhomes could be a hermetic community.

"About his birthday party," Chance explained. "Tuck skipped NA meeting that day and hung out at Randy's party. Bad move."

"Really bad move," Karim shook his head.

"What happened?" I asked. "What are you saying? Tuck never made it back home that night."

"Police raided the party," Karim explained.

"I was there," Ray added. Because of his recidivism, I'd been keeping Tuck on a really short leash. I could no longer suppress my sigh, so frustrated that his demise had happened in my absence.

"Randy and the others got off," Ray continued, "but Tuck was the one with the outstanding warrant. Got locked up again."

"That Randy really derailed my man Tuck—classic innocent victim. Randy was a real menace," asserted Cass, the most intellectual of the group.

"Wrong place, wrong time, wrong guy," elaborated Manny. "I've learned to flee from guys like Randy. They mess you up every time."

I glanced at my outline but decided to let the revelatory discussion flow.

"Tuck went down—it wasn't really what he did but it was who he was with," Zee expounded, to a chorus of gratifying "amens." I thought about summing up by bringing back Ahab but the animated discussion continued to take on a life of its own.

"In the movies, they're called villains, the bad guys," Petie, the Hollywood buff, offered. "In real life, they're troublemakers and stumbling blocks, selfish."

"And they're mean-spirited, selfish, dishonest, manipulative, disrespectful, irresponsible, lazy, greedy, vile, conniving, and violent," Cass took the point and ran with it.

I seized the pause. "Flee the menace!" I exhorted. "Whether it's Micaiah staying away from Ahab, or Tuck staying away from Randy, you have to identify those people that have a negative influence in your life and stay as far away from them as possible."

The unexpected pensiveness pervading the room encouraged me to return to my prepared outline for a point I'd been waiting to interject for a few minutes. "Never underestimate the power of influence. People are typically at the center of life's storms. Relationships can either work for you or against you."

Fence Your Mystery

"What if your Ahab isn't really an Ahab?" Jimmie shouted from the back of the sanctuary.

His question mystified me—not surprising, coming from Jimmie. He was a revolving-door resident—though not quite as bad as Ray—on his second Harkhomes tour of duty, the circumstances of his interval away and reasons for his return still unknown. He seemed on the right path when he moved out several months ago, but his return helped keep my recidivism rate in the stratosphere.

"Jesus said in his Sermon on the Mount, 'They come to you in sheep's clothing, but inwardly they are ferocious wolves,'" offered Tuff, demonstrating that his personal Bible studies were paying off.

"Like in a lot of good movies, you don't know who the bad guy is 'til near the end," Petie chimed in.

"What if the menaces in your life aren't easy to identify?" Cass queried. "They've got a hidden agenda. They're mysterious."

"Figuring out whether someone is a good or bad influence can be tricky sometimes," Chance made clear. "That's what you're talking about right, Jimmie?"

"For me, it was my girlfriend Val," Jimmie confided. "I was just trying to help her out but she tripped me up."

Haltingly, he told the story. Having kicked his drug habit at Harkhomes, he'd saved enough money from his job to get his own room. While his life was coming back together, Val's was coming apart. She lost her job and place. Jimmie let her move in.

"You should've kept your distance," Bert advised.

"Yeah I know. She brought her stuff, smoking in the room, got me back into it . . . well, you see what happened."

"Sometimes you got to put up a fence, man, keep them over there, until you know if they gonna help you or hurt you," Manny said.

"Val was my wolf in sheep's clothing," Jimmie concluded.

"Val was like the old prophet from the Old Testament, the book of First Kings," I jumped in. "Who remembers it?"

"First Kings, chapter thirteen."

"Anybody besides Tuff?"

"The old prophet lied to the young prophet." Les surprised me. Though he couldn't remember what happened, it was a breakthrough getting that much Scripture out of him.

"The young prophet, the man of God from Judah, was deceived by the old prophet," Tuff continued. "He dined with the hypocrite, breaking his fast, then was attacked and killed by a lion on the way home."

"We've had our own deceiver right here in the house." I decided to go back in Harkhomes history for another example. "Were any of you guys here when Bill was a supervisor?"

"I remember him," Ray said. Given he'd been in and out of Hark-homes more than any other resident, I could've have guessed he'd remember Bill. "Dude used to curse us out when you weren't around," Ray continued. "One night I saw him sneaking food out of the fridge after lights out."

"Bill lied to me and I fell for it." I gave them the backstory. When I started Harkhomes, I was desperate for men to volunteer to stay in the shelter overnight so I could get a night off. These volunteers were important because, in addition to a supervisory role, I also expected them to be a role model for the residents. Because I needed the help so badly, I took on Bill as a volunteer, based on his enthusiasm and availability—he had lots of time to give—but without the references I usually required.

"Bill was running a scam," I declared. "He was homeless himself, and 'volunteering' here at the shelter gave him a place to stay. I was clue-less until food and supplies kept coming up missing on his shift. He was truly a wolf in sheep's clothing."

"You needed a fence for Bill," Manny asserted.

"A big, barbed-wire fence for Bill!" Bert added, eliciting some laughter and "amens."

I addressed Jimmie. "Like Tuck, you fell prey to the destructive force of negative association. "But Val was different from Randy. She was not a menace but a mystery. So you didn't have to flee. But you did need to fence, creating and maintaining some degree of separation from a person of dubious influence—a limited association instead of a no association.

"Take it slow with the old prophets." I turned to everyone now. "You must be cautious with the time you spend with people of unknown influ-ence. This is different from your Ahabs, where you need to be extreme."

Gaining momentum, I continued: "This is a more moderate approach, with folks that you're forced to deal with, where a relationship needs to be limited rather than eliminated. Play it safe until the mystery shrouding the person's relationship to you becomes clear: whether the individual is friend or foe. Fence the mystery."

Find Your Mentor
Tuff's hand was up. Since he was one of the few residents who followed this protocol, I quickly recognized him, hoping as always to exalt the standard for others to emulate. Hope springs eternal.

"What if this fleeing and fencing you're talking about causes you to lose a friend?"

"Is someone who jeopardizes your personal progress really a friend?" I questioned back.

You could hear a pin drop—when had that ever happened? I pressed my point.

"Staying away from people who are a negative or dubious influence may not win you any popularity contests or congeniality awards, but you're seeking to gain a victorious lifestyle, not win a bunch of trophies. So get used to it. Decisions you make that move you along your success journey will not please everybody."

The pervasive silence persisted, suggesting that I had struck a rare reflective chord. This was a pivotal moment, so I capitalized to turn the discussion toward my most important point.

"No doubt, relationships can be very complex. But let's try to keep it simple: the people with whom you associate can either make or break you; invest your time in the former; withdraw your time from the latter."

"So what about the people who can make me? Where do you find them? All I got is folks who break."

"Thanks for that question, Chance. It's exactly where I'm going. No one can achieve success going at it alone. Your approach must be inclusive and exclusive: those who support your goals should be included on your team; those who are obstacles to your goals should be excluded from your team. The bottom line is where people stand in relation to your goals. The strategy is simple: distance yourself from people of negative influence; surround yourself with people of positive influence, especially your mentors."

"Can a friend be a mentor?"

Bert's question was perfect, as if I'd planted it. "A mentor is someone you know personally, who gives you practical advice on how to reach your goals, most often a person older than you who has more experiences of life out of which to offer guidance: pastors, coaches, bosses, teachers, guidance counselors, colleagues, concerned relatives, neighbors, devoted volunteers.

"A friend is closer because you are attached to him or her on an emotional level. The support here may be less practical and more spiritual. A friend may contribute to your sense of self by believing in you when nobody else does, validating your values, goals, and convictions by sharing those private thoughts and secret moments, becoming a source of strength by just being there for you.

"There's also the role model, someone whom you may or may not know personally. If you don't know your role model personally, you know enough about his or her life to want to model your life after that person. So a role model is someone you admire, respect, and want to emulate.

"These three categories are not mutually exclusive. One person can play all three roles in your life, first being a role model, then becoming a mentor, and finally a friend, providing positive influence and support all along the way. We have a shining example of the benefits of a mentoring relationship among us."

Inquisitive, the men look around the room at each other, trying to figure out who would be called out.

"Stand up, Elisha." Confusion reigned, since no one in the group went by that name. Chester stood up. Murmurs erupted. "Why am I calling you 'Elisha'?" I asked Chester.

"Because Elisha found his mentor Elijah," he responded.

"What's the key Scripture?"

"'As surely as the Lord lives and as you live, I will not leave you.' Elisha said it to his mentor Elijah three times in Second Kings, chapter two."

"This is the principle of full association, right, Chester?" He nodded. "Can you explain it?"

"Elijah was Elisha's mentor, teaching him the ways of an Old Testament prophet. The day that he died, Elijah wanted to spare his pupil the pain of his imminent departure and three times encouraged him to step away, but the young prophet refused, staying at his mentor's side until the very end."

"And Elisha's persistence paid off," I added. "Right before Elijah was taken up to heaven in a whirlwind and chariots of fire, he granted Elisha the one request he'd made—to have a double portion of Elijah's spirit. Elisha went on to perform twice as many miraculous acts in his ministry as his mentor."

I paused, directing Chester to join me at the front of the sanctuary. "Did you find a mentor, Chester?"

"I found him at church. I like to cook—"

"And you're good at it," Karim interjected, acknowledging the many times Chester had excelled at his Harkhomes cooking duties. Scattered applause affirmed the point.

"I started volunteering in the kitchen at church, spent a lot of time there, starting cooking for after-service fellowship and then for the soup kitchen. The deacon in charge of the soup kitchen liked what I was doing so much that he got me a part-time cooking job in the home of his elderly parents."

"Is the deacon your mentor?" Les asked.

"No, but Mr. Hill, the deacon's dad, is. I'm cooking for him but also helping with the cleaning, gardening, driving, and shopping. Whatever he asks me to do, I'm doing it. So part time is now full time."

"So that's why you ain't 'round here much no more," Steve said.

"Yeah. And he and his wife are retired teachers, so they're helping me study for the GED," Chester smiled.

"What's your extra blessing?" I asked, sharing Chester's smile.

"Mrs. Hill recently had a stroke, so she needs more support. So I'm moving into an empty bedroom in their house so I can be her home attendant in addition to my other duties."

"So you're putting both your joblessness and homelessness behind you because of people of positive influence in your life?" I summarized it with a rhetorical question that brought some of the men excitedly to their feet. His fellow residents each approached him, offering handshakes, high-fives, and bear hugs.

My heart soared with pride. A spontaneous collective celebration was rare. In the past I'd planned out such affirmations, so the authenticity of this moment made it more powerful for me than for them. Watching the congratulatory exchange, I realized that the men themselves had created this milestone through their fellowship, which increased the chances that its impact would be lasting.

I saw tears well up in Chester's eyes. Steve, his best friend, grabbed a clean napkin, wiped them away.

The men formed a huddle around Chester, laid hands on him, and said their Harkhomes cheer: "Bless Chester, Bless Chester, Bless Chester . . ."

Inspired, I summoned the men to remain on their feet. I concluded with a flourish, feeling like it was Sunday morning.

"Who remembers what to do when your Ahab confronts you?"

"You flee," Chance responded.

"You flee from whom?"

Collective contemplation pervaded the room. I prompted further.

"Ahab represents what kind of person?"

"The menace," Zee declared.

"So what do you do when your Ahab confronts you?"

"Flee the menace!"

"When your Randy comes after you?"

"Flee the menace!"

"I can't hear you!"

"FLEE THE MENACE!"

"Now, who remembers what to do when your old prophet confronts you?"

"You play it safe," said Cass.

"You take it slow," offered Bert.

"You put up a fence," proclaimed Chance.

"That's right. You fence. Now, you fence whom? . . . What does the old prophet represent?"

"The hypocrite," said Les.

"Yes, but there's something else I'm looking for . . . What does Val represent here?

"The mystery," Jimmie announced.

"So when you have to deal with your Val, what do you do?"

"Fence the mystery?" Jimmie suggested.

"That's right. When your old prophet comes at you, you—"

"Fence the mystery!" a chorus rang out.

"When your Bill is in the house?"

"Fence the mystery!" all said in unison.

"I can't hear you!"

"FENCE THE MYSTERY!"

"Now, you know what to do when your Elijah's around?"

"Find the mentor." The phrase trickled out.

"When you need some good advice?"

"Find the mentor!" The voices rose together.

"When you need a helping hand?"

"Find the mentor!" they exclaimed in unison.

"What did Chester do?"

"Found the mentor!"

"I can't hear you!

"FOUND THE MENTOR!"

"Now shake somebody's hand and tell him the three things you're going to do to build positive relationships."

As they encouraged one another, I smiled, savoring the victory of this triumphant moment, but my excitement was met with a new challenge very quickly.

"Will you be my mentor?" came flying at me from several men.

I'd become a victim of my own success—it was mission impossible to mentor them all. But I'd rather try to mentor them on the front end than mend them on the back.

Sharpen Your Tools

Nothing has more impact, both positive and negative, in navigating the rapids of life than your interpersonal relationships. Your friends, family, and partners can lift you up, support you, and help you realize your dreams. Or they can hamper you and either unintentionally or purposefully complicate your journey. The key is to understand that you cannot control people. What you *can* control is how you relate to them. The purpose of the *association* tool is to help you manage the people in your life so that they become foundation stones rather than stumbling blocks as you build an inspired life. The following steps will help you develop a lifestyle where your relationships are an asset, not a liability.

Step one: Flee your menace. A menace is someone who is a major distraction, preventing you from making progress toward your goals. If you want to get better at work, at school, at whatever, and there's a person in life who distracts you from getting it done, then keep it simple—create as much distance between you and that person as possible; or, put another way, spend as little time with that person as possible. If you're an athlete and your goal is to get into the best physical shape possible, then the last thing you want to do is to hang around people who are smoking cigarettes, drinking alcohol, and doing drugs, because they might influence you to do the same things. Steer clear of such people, lest they trip you up, breaking your strides of progress, or drag you down into the rut of failure with them. It's trite but true: misery loves company. Lose the losers in your life so that you'll be free to win. Once you've won, you can always go back and show them the way.

Step two: Fence your mystery. Fencing the mystery is a strategy you can use to handle relations with family, coworkers, friends, classmates, colleagues, and significant others who you must deal with out of obligation, tradition, or necessity. The objective is to find a way to manage these relationships in a cautious, circumspect, and self-protective way, so that their necessary presence doesn't become a negative influence. Such people may be a mystery—not obviously destructive but possessing negative traits or character defects that can adversely affect you. Or perhaps the person could be operating in a way that is intentionally deceptive, claiming to help you out when he's really using you to further his own agenda. If so, put up that fence; keep him at a safe distance until you find out if he's friend or foe. I'm not suggesting that you go through life governed by cynicism, suspicious of others' motives, but encouraging you to "look both ways" when faced with decisions about relationships: be careful, wary, circumspect, discerning, and wise. Fence the proverbial wolf in sheep's clothing!

Step three: Find your mentor. No person can achieve success and fulfillment on his or her own. Find a person who builds your confidence, brings encouragement, and sows inspiration into your life. Be creative in finding your mentors. If no one in your "real life" appears, go virtual. Search online for mentors and role models. Explore history for inspirational figures or the contemporary scene for exemplary celebrities or public figures. Books, magazines, movies, plays, TV, the Internet—let the full range of your experience of people, direct and indirect, bring you the positive influences you need to succeed. Once you find a mentor, if he or she is someone who is a part of your life, make time to see that person on a regular basis as time allows and always be honest, courteous, punctual, and respectful. Your mentor is probably taking time away from other priorities to spend time with you, so be careful to honor that commitment. Go out of your way to show how much you appreciate your mentor: be early for appointments; come prepared with written questions or updates; have meetings at the place of greatest convenience; don't make contact at awkward or inopportune times; and from time to time, send a thank-you note or a letter updating your progress.

Step four: Fortify your family. Family is the foundational relationship, so don't sacrifice your family for your career. Instead, make your family relationships a priority, fostering stability and togetherness rather than fragmentation and tension. Cultural trends cut against this commitment. Divorce rates are up, marriage rates are down, and single parenthood is more prevalent than ever before. Statistics demonstrate that single parenthood is a decision that places potentially huge barriers blocking not only your success—kids in such households are several times as likely as children from married-couple families to live in poverty. This is not intended to be a judgment against single parents because many endeavor to create a healthy home environment for their children. One of the most important—and inspirational—things you can do in life is be a good parent to your child, and beyond that, a good uncle to your nephew; a niece to your aunt; a sibling to your sibling, and so on. Strong family relationships can be mutually uplifting, even life changing! Be the biggest fan of your child or other family member, becoming the bulwark in the hearth against the storms outside the door.

Step five: Forgive your team. At one point or another, you will be hurt emotionally by others, even by those closest to you—it is inevitable in life. Spouses, friends, coworkers, relatives, classmates, fellow church members, business partners, and even mentors will let you down. You may even feel betrayed at times. Staying hurt and mired in anger is your choice. Don't do it. Offer mercy to those who have hurt you. If you seek reconciliation and offer forgiveness, you will stop the cycle of reprisal, reboot the relationship, and initiate a cycle of good. But if you're living with blame, bitterness, and hate, you erect a spiritual barrier blocking grace and favor from flowing into your life. Face the fact that most people are not for you or against you; they are most concerned about themselves. Acknowledge that your team is made up of flawed human beings that will sometimes make mistakes. Forgive—lead them back into the huddle of healing.

ASSOCIATION AFFIRMATION

I will flee the menace, having no association with people of negative influence; I will fence the mystery, having limited association with people of dubious influence; and I will find the mentor, having full association with people of positive influence.

TOOL #6

PLANNING
THE PENCIL
BUILDING PRIORITIES

The parole officer's visit was unexpected. It was even more surprising that he asked for Chip, my star resident. "He's at work," I informed the officer. Chip was working part time at a construction site, studying part time at a Harlem-based college, about to become a member of his church, and had even been appointed an assistant supervisor at Harkhomes. When a local newspaper featured the work of Harkhomes, Chip's story was the lead and his picture appeared along with the article.

"This is how I knew he was here," explained the parole officer, showing me that news article, informing me that Chip was in violation of his parole, proving that not all publicity is good publicity. As our conversation continued, I got more and more fed up with his attitude. He talked as if my men were riffraff, underserving of a second chance.

"Don't you know that in the eyes of God, every weed is a potential rose and every loser a potential winner?" I challenged him as he hung around waiting for Chip to show up.

"I'm just doing my job," he snorted, towing Chip away that very afternoon, my pleas notwithstanding. Sent back to jail, Chip was derailed. I never saw him again.

I had trouble sleeping that night, upset over the loss of one of my exemplary men. I prayed and searched the scriptures for answers. One thing became clear: if Chip had told me about his parole situation, we could have put together a plan to address the situation. I would have been able to intervene with the authorities on his behalf and have him assigned to my supervision, as I had done for other residents with the same problem. But he failed to let me know about this fateful detail. In his drive to get ahead, he neglected it.

Reckon with Your Ghosts

The question arose immediately in morning fellowship: "What happened to Chip?" In addition to disclosing the actual facts, I read a verse that I'd discovered a few hours earlier—"The foolish ones took their lamps but did not take any oil with them. The wise ones, however, took oil in jars along with their lamps" (Matthew 25:3–4).

I established the spiritual context for Chip's demise through Jesus's parable of the ten virgins who were waiting for the bridegroom. The five virgins described as "wise" had taken an extra supply of oil along with them; the five described as "foolish" had not. When the bridegroom came, the wise virgins, having made preparations ahead of time, were ready to go with him.

"But the lamps of the foolish ones had gone out," I expounded. "They were scurrying around at the last minute looking for more oil. When they finally returned, it was too late. Opportunity had passed them by: the bridegroom had come and gone!"

I knew my take on this passage was a stretch. Its traditional interpretation concerned the second coming of Christ, of which no one in my half-awake audience seemed to be aware. But my goal was to use the story to highlight the importance of planning.

"The first virgins were wise because they managed well the precious resource called time, packing extra oil ahead of time. They were ready to seize the opportunity when it came, while their unprepared counterparts missed the proverbial boat. This parable is about planning as the decisive factor between squandering and maximizing opportunities."

"Chip was no fool," Wayne remarked. "It was just bad luck—the *Daily News* story did him in. You should've put me in the paper instead of him."

Now this is a first, I thought to myself. My men had blamed me for a lot of things, but never before for a wrong publicity choice.

"Get over it, Wayne," Rap quipped. "You upset 'cause Chip made the paper instead of you, and Rev not putting you in the paper 'cause you never pick your fro." A comb flew at Wayne as laughter filled the room. As usual, my elucidations were less effective at engaging them than their own banter. I pressed on.

"Chip's problem was that he wasn't prepared. His myopia fore-doomed his rise." Why did I say that? The whispers and grumbles meant that I'd missed the mark with my Ivy League vocabulary yet again. *At least it doesn't happen as often these days*, I consoled myself. I tried a more straightforward explanation.

"You must get ready in advance of the opportunity because of the uncertain timing of life. It wasn't clear to any of the virgins when the bridegroom would arrive. You just don't know when opportunity will knock. Like the bridegroom, it may be a long time in coming. You don't want to be scurrying around at the last minute trying to get yourself together and end up missing out."

"The ghost got Chip."

Lincoln's declaration riveted the room.

"A ghost got him with old baggage."

I liked his analogy, even his mix of metaphors. So did the brothers, evidenced by the exclamations of "Deep, deep," "Word up," and "You da man."

"Ghosts of the past come back," Lincoln continued. "They haunt your present and your future."

Somebody made a silly joke about wearing ghost costumes at a

Harkhomes Halloween party. I endeavored to recapture the crowd with a catchy phrase I'd been saving for my climax: "First you plan to work, then you work the plan."

I surrendered after another lousy joke about ghosts haunting Harkhomes on check day and closed the session in prayer: "Lord, help the men of this house take your truth seriously and apply it to their lives." I'd given up on my ability alone to get them to pay attention.

That evening, I summoned Lincoln to the office. He hailed from South Carolina, and had the distinctive drawl to prove it. A bright guy with a paralegal certificate, he'd left to escape the heartache of a bitter divorce, hoping life in the Big Apple would bring brighter days. He'd found just the opposite: work was hard to find without references; he began hanging with the wrong crowd; and he relapsed into bad habits of drinking and womanizing. Eventually he was kicked out of the house by fair-weather relatives and ended up homeless.

"You got any ghosts?" I asked him.

Before he could answer the question, Ray suddenly rushed through the door, perspiring, panting—terror in his eyes.

"What's wrong?" I asked him, but he was too petrified to speak. I hurried past him outside to the sidewalk. All was quiet. The only thing that caught my eye was a big black man walking slowly away from the shelter.

I returned inside, perplexed about Ray's condition. "Where is he?" I asked Lincoln.

"In the bathroom," he responded. "You were talking to me about ghosts. He looked like he'd seen one."

"You're right about that," I affirmed. "He looked really scared. But let's get back to *your* ghosts. I'll find out about Ray's ghosts later."

"Got a big one. Worse than Chip's," he responded. He explained that he'd violated the order of protection that his ex-wife had against him. She was harassing him for support payments that he didn't have; he'd lost his temper and assaulted her. He'd fled north to avoid arrest.

"Why didn't you tell me this before?"

"All I wanted was to be as far away as possible from home and my problems there. And I was afraid you'd turn me in. Now I'm more afraid I might end up like Chip"

I hesitated, pondering my moral dilemma. Lincoln was a fugitive on the run from a violent crime; but he was also a needy soul who'd just confessed his need for my help.

"What are you going to do?" I asked him. "You need a plan."

"A plan for my ghosts?"

"You can't ignore or outrun the ghosts of the past. They will always catch up with you."

We decided on a course of action. Once he showed evidence of progress, I'd contact the South Carolina correctional authorities on his behalf. But I discovered that there was no similar policy to remand an offender like him to a program like mine.

Feeling hopeless and frustrated, Lincoln continued to just go through the motions at Harkhomes, nodding through my morning teachings, in denial about his role in the tornado of circumstances that had overturned his life. Out of the blue one morning, Lincoln informed me that he was returning to South Carolina.

I counseled him to take a little more time to prepare for the demands of his homecoming, but he was adamant.

"What about the ghosts?" I challenged him.

"C'mon, Rev, you really believe in ghosts?" He borrowed enough money for a bus ticket and headed home.

Ride on Your Ground

"Run into any ghosts down South?" I asked a humbled Lincoln, who was standing on the Harkhomes doorstep less than a month later. His was a sad but all too predictable story. Without job or money, he bounced around nightly between friends and family upon his return to South Carolina. Without the résumé or wardrobe to job hunt, he borrowed survival money from his fraying network, some of whom treated him like a pariah, the last thing this defeated man needed.

Inevitably, his ex-wife's brother spotted him, the police pounced, and Lincoln landed in jail. No bail money led to him spending a couple of days behind bars, driving him to write a suicide note. Fortunately his uncle, a well-placed politician, facilitated his release and suspended sentence— and, at Lincoln's request, bought him a bus ticket to return to New York.

"Why'd you come back here?" I asked him, hoping he was finally ready to take his head out of the sand.

"It was a long bus ride north," he admitted.

"What did you do?"

"Ripped up my suicide note."

"That's a start," I offered. "Any other decisions?"

"I need some oil in my lamp."

His evocation of Jesus's parable stunned me. It got better.

"I tried to sleep during the ride but couldn't," he reflected. "I believed I was leaving my ghosts behind but knew that wasn't enough. Then the bus stopped, dropped off passengers, picked some up." He paused, as if still in the moment.

"Then the bus started up again, 'til the next stop. The driver had a plan. He stuck to the plan. There was an accident—road closed. Driver made a detour but then got back on route, sticking to his plan.

"A passenger got sick. We made an emergency stop. Ambulance came. Driver got right back on the road. He stuck to the plan, whatever came up, all the way to Port Authority."

He pulled out a crumpled sheet of paper with lots of scratched-out scribbles. "I wrote some stuff down. I need to ride like that driver. Keep it real all the way. I need a plan for today . . . for tomorrow . . . for every day."

He showed me his notes, which were hard to understand with all the crossed-out words and between-the-line insertions. I suggested that he rewrite them and handed him paper and pen. He refused them.

"I need a pencil."

"Why a pencil?" I queried, searching the desk in vain for one.

"Look at this mess." He held up his old notes. "With a pencil I can keep working with the plan, changing it, adding, erasing, shaping it, until I get it right."

Since he was insistent about the pencil, we asked around Hark-homes until a stub with a well-worn eraser was produced. He used a kitchen knife to whittle at the edge until the dull point became fine. "You can make a pencil your own thing, just as you like it," he marveled, admiring his handiwork.

He began to rewrite his plan of action, erasing as much as marking, writing then stopping, then starting again. He was no longer mired in his past but was riding on the ground like the bus driver, plotting purposefully toward his destination. When he ran out of paper, I quickly went to get him some more.

Reach for Your Glory

Lincoln's writings were more like journal entries than agenda notes. The depth of his musings surprised me, proving that he hadn't slept through every one of my Bible lessons. He acknowledged his anger problem, surveyed his insecurities, and confessed that his violent eruptions had foredoomed his marriage. He rejected the blame game he'd been playing and the self-pity he'd been wallowing in. And he even quoted some Scripture—a rare feat for which I rewarded him with fewer chores.

I advised him to write a plan of action for each day. "You must develop a plan, determining the actions to take to achieve your objectives. Then you develop a schedule to manage your time as you pursue your goals." He not only accepted my counsel but suggested he do his planning the night before. "This is the hard part," I told him. "Making plans with priorities and deadlines and sticking to them. You must hold yourself accountable in accordance with your priorities."

Lincoln was diligent but diffuse in his planning for what his future held. His thinking was all over the place: from acting to engineering to starting a business to singing opera to playing in a jazz band.

"You've got to prioritize your plan," I counseled.

"Not sure how to prioritize."

"You only have twenty-four hours in a day. You can't do everything, so you do the most important things. You must develop your daily plan based on the unique factors of your situation in light of what's needed to reach your goal. If you were a recovering drug addict like Mack, you go through detoxification before taking any other steps."

"Or a high-school dropout like Frankie," he added. "Needs to get his GED before he looks for a job."

"Exactly. First things first."

"How do you figure out the first things?"

"Reach for the glory. Plan with the end in mind, concentrating on destiny and working back from there to what needs to be done right now to create that future. Go after the thing that you care most about. Decide on that—your destination. Then you make your plans and set your priorities to get you there."

"Like the bus driver getting me to New York."

"That's right!" I affirmed, thinking about the same analogy and thrilled that he discovered it without my prompting. "Make sure you have a glory plan."

"This place isn't such a glorious destination," he demurred, raining on my parade.

"You prefer Miami?" I quipped.

"Charleston's my city," he declared.

"You're not ready to go back home," I warned.

"Okay," he agreed. "Not yet, but one of these days."

"Don't rush it this time."

Despite my admonitions, Lincoln clung to his goal to go back home. He dreamed of becoming an engineer, building housing in his favorite city, Charleston. So I helped him think strategically about moving through his present plight towards his future plans. He found a part-time dishwashing job, got into a community college course at night to earn credits towards his degree, and attended a workshop on anger management and emotional pain. He even arranged some one-on-one Q-and-A sessions with one of our volunteers who worked as an engineer for a construction company.

Lincoln had to revise his plans when he was promoted to waiting tables at the restaurant. He wisely accepted the assignment and the income boost from sharing tips, but he had to adjust his school schedule to an independent study since he had less time to attend class.

As he executed his daily plan of action, Lincoln's emotional fog lifted. He now saw more clearly the collateral consequences of his choices, so he came to me with a change of plans.

"I'm ready to go back," he asserted.

"When?"

"Now?"

"Are you sure?"

He explained his reasoning. When he'd left South Carolina, he had run away—not only from a destructive relationship, but also from going to school at night to attain his engineering degree. He had also left important support networks—his family, friends, school cronies, coworkers, and church members—that helped him balance school and work.

"I can take the money I've saved to get a room around here," he spelled out, "and use it on my priority—to get started again back home. Isn't this a way for me to reach for the glory?"

He'd convinced me that this was a better plan, more in line with his aspirations. Whereas before his choice was a reactionary flight from his problems, this time he made the decision to return to Charleston fully aware of the potential pitfalls, but also cognizant that it was his best hope of attaining the academic and career goals he had now set for himself.

Taking a completely different approach to this homecoming, Lincoln planned ahead, making this return a much more manageable prospect. He made calls back home to gather information about his job and housing prospects; registered for night school; and corresponded with family members and friends to mend fences and build bridges for a broader base of support that would cushion him against the circumstances from which he had twice taken flight. He scheduled additional counseling sessions in order to prepare himself to handle unexpected emotional encounters. He triumphantly paid for his own bus ticket this time around.

A few weeks after Lincoln's departure, a package came from him. I quickly opened it and ripped open the letter, eager as I was to hear how he was faring. Staying with his cousins, he'd been working two part-time jobs while rebuilding his wardrobe and preparing to reapply for his old job as a personnel supervisor. His relevant experience and new attitude regained him the position. And he was still reaching for the glory, taking courses at night.

There was also in Lincoln's package a box of pencils, with a note: *These are for the guys. Tell them to start planning.*

Attached to the pencils was a small plastic sharpener, with a note: *This is for you. To keep them sharp. And remind the brothers: "First plan to work. Then work the plan."*

During evening fellowship, I first read a letter of Lincoln's testimony. Amazement filled the room.

"Lincoln has a message for each of you."

I passed index cards around to them all and had each man read the words I'd written on the cards: *First plan to work. Then work the plan.*

"Lincoln also sent a gift to you guys."

I gave them the pencils, explaining their significance by recounting the moment, which some remembered, when Lincoln sharpened his stub of a pencil to write his first plan of action. The silence of awe pervaded the room.

"Lincoln also sent this." I held up the sharpener. "Now, to honor Lincoln's example, let's get ready to plan."

The sharpener was passed from man to man around the table. While the others watched, each man sharpened his own pencil. The solemnity of the ceremony inspired Rob to declare his intention to return to GED class and Tune to promise to write a letter to his mother for the first time. I kept one of Lincoln's pencils for myself. The next morning I sharpened it. I've been using a pencil—with a fine point— to plan ever since.

Sharpen Your Tools

If you fail to plan, you plan to fail. Keep this in mind as you forge a mindset that will allow you to strategically address past, present, and future issues with the *planning tool.* This tool blends time management tactics with crisis management principles, enhancing your ability to manage short-term objectives while pursuing long-term goals. No matter how crazy life seems, following these steps will help you bring order to your agendas, identify your priorities, and lay out your road map for the journey ahead.

Step one: Reckon with your ghosts. Plan with the past in mind. Pay attention to the consequences—financial, legal, relational, emotional—of your past. Address the breakdowns that happened yesterday, last week, last month, last year, in your youth, whenever. Think exhaustively about it. Leave no stone unturned. This is your cleanup plan. It might feel a lot easier to leave your mess buried in the past than to resurrect the unpleasant stuff and figure out how to straighten it out. Don't risk it. You ignore the old things at your peril. Reckon with your ghosts. As the philosopher George Santayana memorably wrote: "Those who cannot remember the past are condemned to repeat it." Work on your cleanup plan—the bigger the prior breakdowns, the greater the need for it. If you don't, ghosts from your past will show up to haunt your present and your future.

Step two: Rule with practicality. Take charge of your day. Refuse to be distracted by drudgery, frivolity, and worry. Set your agenda and stick to it. You determine your future by your daily routine. Develop good habits and do them day after day. In this way you are creating for yourself a bright future. Plan ahead of time. Make a weekly schedule and follow through on it. List the tasks on your agenda at the beginning of the week and monitor your progress each day. Make sure you set deadlines—and keep them. Be consistent with day-by-day agenda setting, hour-by-hour scheduling, and minute-by-minute prioritizing. Setting your priorities means you'll get to the most important things first, which is essential because you'll never have enough time to do everything you want or need to do. Sometimes you have to refuse to take on tasks until you've completed the ones you must do. Hold yourself accountable as you manage your time. If you commit to these good practices and habits, your goals will come to pass.

Step three: Realize the time is now. Treat time as the most precious commodity there is. Procrastination is a ruthless thief of time, robbing you of opportunities to take daily steps toward progress. When you procrastinate, you believe—mistakenly—that you'll have time to do it later; in the meantime, life happens, and you never get to it or you get to it too late. Then you get stressed out and burned out by scurrying around at the last minute when you don't have enough time to get it done with excellence. Live in the present as much as possible and make the most of it. Don't be idle when you could be productive. Industry is what powers the journey to your future. The longer you delay, the further away your dreams will remain.

Step four: Review your game plan. Be flexible. I once heard a preacher say, "Never start your day until you have finished it." His point was to set a regular time to review your plan of action. On any given day, do it early—before sunrise, maybe even the night before—so you can make changes to your schedule, adjust your priorities, revise strategies in accordance with the realities as they emerge. Don't trust your memory. Have a notebook handy for those unanticipated moments in those unexpected places. Keep a written record of important thoughts, a folder for upcoming events. Refer to it as much as you need to, delete less important happenings, and plug in new priorities. Be diligent about writing stuff down. One of the worst feelings is to forget a revelation that would have propelled you and others. Always have your pencil handy! With a good eraser!

Step five: Reach for your glory. Find the purpose for your life. Be vigilant about fathoming the larger meaning for your life. If you're still looking for it, look deeper within. Reach for your glory by delving inside your soul and spirit. Don't neglect your inner life. Are you so preoccupied with work and family obligations, with hobbies and social life, that you've left no time for the prayer pillow, the contemplative closet, those meditative moments of solitude when you can get in touch with the inner you? Make a devotional plan. Set a time every day to be by yourself: to pray, to journal, to study your Bible, to read your sacred text, to think about how you can evolve more and more into the person of your dreams. By observing a period of solitude and devotion every day, you will build inspiration for your life. And you will bring glory into your life. It will become the best time of your day.

PLANNING AFFIRMATION

I will execute a cleanup plan, preventing ghosts from my past from haunting my present and future; I will implement a daily plan of action, setting priorities and deadlines and sticking to them; and I will create a glory plan, dreaming big and working hard every day to realize my dream.

TOOL #7

WORK

THE COMPASS
BUILDING INTEGRITY

What Harlem needed was ice cream. Opening a franchise of Ben & Jerry's in the neighborhood had been my inspiration, pitched to a Ben & Jerry's executive who'd heard me speak during my Vermont trip. I'd sensed a win-win-win: jobs for my hard-to-employ strivers; a new business to strike a commercial blow against the community's cycles of disinvestment and unemployment; and luster to the company's social mission.

The newly opened shop at the corner of 125th Street and 5th Avenue—the very heart of Harlem—featured hanging lamps, mahogany booths, pressed-tin ceiling, ceramic tile floors, soda fountain–style counter, and a bucolic wall of grazing Holstein cows—a throwback Harlem Renaissance look with New England patina; a bucolic slice of life sandwiched by urban dreams.

I hand-selected some of the Harkhomes men to staff the shop. My plan was to transform them from the ranks of the unemployed into champion scoopers. For the first year, we had been meeting once a week so that I could drill the crew in customer service fundamentals.

I'd really seen the experiment as less a job than an internship, to re-engage them with the workforce, as a stepping-stone to real-world responsibilities. It'd also been for me an opportunity to test my philosophy of holistic work: work as the combination of character development and work ethic. I'd been teaching these attributes at Harkhomes but I envisaged an operating business as an ideal environment to prove that I could equip my hard-to-employ men with integrity and good employable habits.

My initial confidence had been buoyed by the media, which hailed my initiative. *People, Fortune, Time, Black Enterprise*, the *New York Times*, and the *Wall Street Journal* all ran stories, while the *Daily News* called me a "folk hero."

The exception to the puff pieces was the *New York Post*, whose cartoon lampooned my optimistic enterprise as a fool's errand. Who knew that the jaded perspective would prove prophetic?

"Do you really want to open a pricey, offbeat ice cream shop staffed by homeless men in the heart of America's most famous ghetto?" was a common question hurled my way in various forms in the run-up to the store's opening.

I was unfazed by all the buzz and doubters in my zeal to create jobs in Harlem, where unemployment rates had long been more than thrice the rate of the rest of New York City, and much higher when it came to the black men who populated my staff. It was so tough to get them employed that I decided to employ them myself.

But $1.75 for a super-premium ice cream scoop was a hard sell, especially if you were collecting government assistance, which was the situation for 50 percent of my potential customers—a market assessment about how to bring an upscale product into a downscale community I somehow glossed over in my zealousness.

What loomed as an even greater problem than the uncooperative marketplace was my intractable staff. Who knew that scooping ice cream would be a herculean task? My early enthusiasm for the initiative had melted quickly in the crucible of daily operations, like an ice cream cone in the swelter of a summer day.

My preaching shifted from "Read your Bible!" to "The customer is always right!" But with the prevalence of displeased patrons, my crusading about customer service seemed just as fruitless as my pep talks about probity. There was one counterintuitive upside: with robberies raging in Harlem, a crew of ex-cons behind the counter made us the rare 125th Street business untouched by crime. I was trying to focus on the positive.

Foster Your Character

As we approached the first anniversary of the venture, it was increasingly clear that deficiencies in inventory control, cash management, and service protocols threatened to overwhelm the business. I'd been harping on those issues so much that I'd decided to focus this morning's weekly staff issue on a favorite theme that had proven so elusive to my staff: the holistic nature of work.

In putting this talk together, I had one guy particularly in mind—Nate. Because of his good looks, personality, and gift of gab, I'd harbored hopes of Nate becoming our Super Scooper. But I underestimated the extreme challenge of converting a thirtysomething street hustler who'd never worked a regular job in his life into a workaday person. He earned the nickname Nate the Over-Scooper, for refusing to cut back on the over-generous ice cream portions he provided each customer.

Nate had lived by the welfare ethic, stretching his government assistance as far as possible, supplementing it with various schemes: selling drugs, bootlegging, running numbers, playing the doctors. So he had no notion of a standard work ethic: holding down a job, getting to work on time, applying himself to an assigned task, submitting to a supervisor, being accountable, cooperating with coworkers.

Nate had his hands full just dealing with these workplace fundamentals, but this challenge was compounded by his character deficiencies. Recently, he really turned out to be his own worst enemy. During a cigarette break in front of the store, he flirted with a young female customer to whom he'd just sold a cone. He followed her down the block as she flirted back. He didn't come back to work that day, or the next day, and didn't call in.

This sort of periodic backsliding was characteristic of his fellow employees, but Nate was the most unreliable of them. I thought about firing him, but my practice of tough love typically missed the tricky balance of hard and soft consequences and erred on the tenderhearted side. *Blessed are the merciful*—I kept encouraging myself with Jesus's Sermon on the Mount directive, but my guys kept exploiting my kindness for weakness.

When he was in the wrong, Nate liked to deflect the focus. "C'mon, Rev, you got to admit that I wasn't as bad as Ray," comparing himself favorably with my most intractable resident. I'd decided to give Ray a chance scooping at Ben & Jerry's, but after a week of him gone AWOL, I had to fire him. Even with my boundless optimism, I was beginning to wonder, *Will Ray ever get himself together?*

Nate also blamed his lapse on bad luck. If the sexy customer hadn't hung around outside the store—if she had left right away—he would've been okay. "From now on, I'm serving cross-eyed old ladies with no teeth," he joked. His faulty reasoning focused on the timing of his flawed decision rather than the character flaw that gave rise to it. But he agreed to change his ways, and I reluctantly welcomed him back to the staff, hoping for—yet still doubting—the genuineness of his change.

As I gathered with half a dozen restless men for the staff meeting around the largest table in the shop, right under a large mural of cows looking down over the proceedings, Nate was as usual the late one. Stalling for time and looking to enliven my languid listeners, I yet again attempted a joke. (Would I ever learn?) "What would Ben & Jerry have called their most popular flavor Cherry Garcia if they had named if after the Godfather of Soul James Brown instead of the rock legend Jerry Garcia?" . . . "Funky Cherry!"

Amidst the groans arose "Stick to preaching, Rev," which I happily used to segue to the opening prayer. Though the humor failed, the stalling tactic worked, as Nate arrived just in time for the day's scriptural role model, the great Old Testament leader Nehemiah, who was called by God to rebuild the wall of Jerusalem after his people returned from Babylonian exile. The rebuilding came under military attack by those opposed to their movement back.

"How many years ago was this?" Slick yawned.

"About twenty-four hundred years, but Nehemiah preached a timeless truth," I insisted, reaching for relevance. "Continue to build the wall, but you also have to fight to defend the wall. So they used a hammer in one hand to keep building the wall while holding a shield in the other hand to protect the wall."

"So what does this have to do with scooping ice cream?" Nate queried, ever the contrarian.

"The hammer symbolizes career work—that which you do to earn a living. The shield symbolizes character work—that which you do to foster virtue. You need both to succeed.

"Career work elevates your job and produces resources." I stared down Nate with this next point. "The key for you is to work harder on your character than you do your career, to keep from becoming your own worst enemy."

"Why you looking at me, Rev?" Nate fired back at me.

"You're not alone. We all have flaws, weaknesses, shortcomings that lead to bad choices. You guys say, 'Get me a job and I'll be okay.' But your character work must precede career work. How many guys do you know who got some work, messed up, lost it?"

Hands went up, along with some nods. Nate sat motionless.

"You need to work really hard at correcting your flaws and strengthening your weaknesses so they won't trip you up on the job. So you won't become your own worst enemy. Like letting sexy customers keep you from getting to work." I looked pointedly at Nate.

"Low blow!" and "Ouch!" among other commentary rang out as I concluded. Not happy as the object of derision, Nate glared at me. Had I finally really gotten his attention?

A couple of customers were at the door, so a quick prayer ended the session and we got to work.

Later that day in the store's basement office, as I agonized over how to reconcile receipts with the register tape (which always proved elusive), Nate knocked on my door, which was different since he typically barged in.

"On my break," he explained, another novelty, since he rarely explained anything.

"Here to beat me up over making you an object lesson this morning?" I asked.

Nate hesitated, nervously running his fingers through his dreads. "I need to talk about this worst enemy thing . . ."

"Integrity is a choice. You have to work really hard at doing the right thing because decisions are not made in a moment in time but they're rooted in character."

"What about you—you always do the right thing?

"No, I mess up. I'm a sinner saved by grace. Thank God I'm getting better every day. The Lord can help you, too."

"Can you keep it real, Rev? How'd you mess up?"

I reflected, searching for a personal truth with which I could make a meaningful connection. "Once, when I was in school, studying for exams, word came through a football teammate that he had secured a copy of the answers to the upcoming economics final. I had a choice to make: study or cheat. I wavered at first but then I got to thinking about the time I would save to use for other subjects and how I could get a high grade in my worst subject."

"Really, Rev? Cheating on a test? What about whether to snatch a purse to get money to eat? Or jumping the subway turnstile to get home to your baby momma? Or beating up the guy who raped your sister? Or lying to stay out of jail?"

Nate had a point—his troubled past yielded moral dilemmas that trivialized my own quandaries. This was the hard part for me. My relatively privileged upbringing made me a lousy role model at these moments. Since nothing in my history was as dire as the circumstances and choices that confronted him and my spiritual encouragement had fallen flat, I tried a metaphor.

"I admit you came up the side of the mountain that was steeper and rockier than my side of the mountain,"

"C'mon, Rev, where you going with this? I ain' been on a mountain trail an' got no plans to go hiking."

"You need a moral compass, Nate," I offered, switching gears. "Your life is a series of decisions, of roads traveled and roads not traveled—a long string of choices, where you can take one path or another. Life is about making these choices. Your moral compass points you toward the right decisions and away from the wrong ones."

"You makin' no sense, man."

"Have you ever heard of the Ten Commandments?"

"You're back to Bible again?"

"Not murdering, lying, coveting, lusting, stealing—those are all on your compass. Obeying those simple rules will keep you off the wrong road that leads to trouble." I paused to let this truth settle, hoping the last two injunctions would hit home. Nate was not only guilty of sexy customer seductions but was also my chief suspect for missing register money.

"Not getting this, Rev."

"Set your compass for the high road." I leaned in for emphasis. "Honesty, integrity, just doing what you know is right, just keeping your word, just being on time for work—this is little stuff, but it leads to big rewards."

"Life ain' that simple," Nate sighed.

"You're right. Life is more gray than black-and-white. Sometimes it's hard to tell which path is the better one to follow, but that's why you carry and check your moral compass. It's all about being aware of your conscience and developing the quality of mind and heart to guide you to sound decisions, to make right choices. It's an every day, every hour, every second thing. To get it right, it takes work . . . hard work . . . on yourself."

"How you set this compass?"

"There's no set formula, no one right way. It happens in a lot of ways. I do it by praying, reading the Bible, going to church, reading biographies and classic literature, being a student of my life and the lives of others. Pay attention to what's good and true and noble going on around you—you'll know it when you see it—and do it."

"Nate, you're up!" The voice rang out from outside the office, signaling the end of his break. Glad to escape my glare, Nate retook his position behind the ice cream–stocked glass counter in record time. Was this a first step toward a new conscientiousness?

During my periodic checks the rest of the day, I discreetly observed Nate taking more time to ensure the expected amount of scoop made it to the cone. And I was encouraged that, at the end of his shift, the cash in the register reconciled to the tape—to the penny!

Forge Your Career

During a meeting with a marketing consultant whom I was interviewing to help spur our lackluster sales, a loud behind-the-counter conversation drew my attention.

"No, I don't want the Harlem Bluesberry," insisted the customer. "I said I want the rum raisin."

"I can't serve you the rum raisin," responded Mitt, one of my best scoopers.

Excusing myself, I slipped from behind the large table and headed toward the counter.

"Why not?" demanded the customer. "I'm looking at the rum raisin right there."

"It has alcohol in it," Mitt explained.

Before I could intervene, Nate, the co-server on the shift, deftly maneuvered between Mitt and the irate customer, explaining that the rum in the ice cream was only used for flavoring. As he scooped the ice cream, Nate explained that Mitt, a recovering substance abuser, was "a little sensitive" in his quest to prevent others from going down the path he'd been on. He then offered the cone gratis for any inconvenience.

I was stunned. I'd noted over the past few weeks his on-time attendance for shifts and meetings as a change in the right direction, but Nate's display of textbook customer service warmed me like a Miami breeze in a Vermont snowstorm.

I wasn't the only one Nate had impressed. "Are you the store manager?" asked the next customer in line. I explained I was the owner. "Who is that server?" He pointed at Nate. After my description of the store's missions and Nate's attributes, which I sugarcoated—perhaps a little too much—he fired another question: "Does Nate have a résumé?"

I hedged the answer (which was no), already plotting that Nate and I could put together a résumé quickly. I sought Nate out during his break. "You really impressed that customer. He gave me his card. He's an entrepreneur opening a new clothing store looking for the right sales staff, and he likes your look, style, and customer service. I told you you even get to work on time."

"Good thing I've been using my compass." He pulled out a pocket Bible and small notebook. "But which way do I point to find a résumé?"

"As long as you got your compass with you, we'll find it. Come see me after your shift."

Downstairs in the office later that day, I handed Nate a copy of the model résumé that I used for occasions like this.

"What do I do now?" Nate wondered, staring at the one-pager.

"It's a point on your compass," I explained. "Use this résumé as a guide to create your own. Refer to it for form, using your own informa-tion to write your first draft. Remember to get to the point right away, and avoid sentences. You're writing for someone to scan, not read. If it's too long, he may not even look at it."

"Don't worry about too long. I only have this job to put down," he said, a worried look on his face. "Why can't you just write it up for me?"

"Don't get lazy on me. It's *your* résumé for *your* job application. *You* must do it."

"Can you at least type for me?"

"We'll cross that bridge when we get to it. First things first."

"You got paper?" he sighed. I handed him several sheets. He pulled out a pencil—a Harkhomes policy since the days of Lincoln—made room on the edge of my desk, and got to work.

It was a long and arduous process. His questions were endless. "Should I put down I'm still working on my GED? . . . Should I use the Harkhomes or Ben & Jerry's address? . . . C'mon, Rev, can't you just do it for me? . . . How do you spell 'experience'? . . . Does our copier work? . . . Okay, but who's the best guy to proofread? . . . I once had a job shining shoes. Does that count? . . ."

A few days and countless drafts later, we had an acceptable résumé and cover letter. Nate waited anxiously for me to type it, made copies, and rushed out to deliver it.

The next day the good news came: Nate got an interview, coming up in a couple days. As soon as the call came in, he tracked me down, notebook in hand. "I'm ready," he said expectantly.

"Good, because you got a lot of work to get ready and not much time to do it," I responded.

"Got my compass," he held up the notebook.

I handed him another one-pager. "Here's your checklist of things to do to be ready for your interview."

"You gotta be kiddin', Rev. All this stuff?!"

"Do you want the job or not?"

"What do I do?"

"You know what to do."

"Will you help me with the to-do list?"

"What do you think?"

He grabbed a sheet of paper and his pencil.

"Get focused," I said. "I don't have all day like with the résumé."

He fired his questions more quickly this time. "What should I wear? . . . Can I borrow a tie? . . . What about your pinstriped suit? . . . Can I talk about the time I saved the rum raisin customer? . . . Should I talk about the time I got arrested? . . . Do I really need to lose my dreads? . . . How much time do I have to answer each question? . . .What you tryin' to say, Rev, I talk a lot? . . . Do I have any relevant education or training to describe? Relevant work experience? Does this job count? . . . Can I borrow your deodorant? . . . What salary should I ask for? . . . Should I cut my nails? . . . Can I use one of our smiley cow cards for the thank-you note?"

Given his rising motivation, the interview prep took less time than the résumé prep. With his fresh haircut and borrowed suit and tie, Nate really looked the part. I waited at the scoop shop for his return the afternoon of the interview. His droopy shoulders weren't a good sign.

"You didn't get the job?" I feared to ask the question.

"Almost," he replied despondently.

"You have to go back?"

"I need a reference letter."

"So I'll write you one."

"Not from you—the boss said."

Now I understood his mood.

"Where do I get a reference letter?" he anguished.

"Where's your compass?"

I asked him the question to buy time as I thought quickly whether I had anyone in my network who would write Nate such a letter; I came up empty.

"Already checked it. You gave me nothing on reference letter."

So I resorted to an age-old source that had never let me down.

"Did I ever tell you about 'the ram in the bush'?"

"Don't remember that one."

"It's an Old Testament reference. In Genesis chapter twenty-two, Abraham finds an unexpected blessing to save the day—a ram caught in a thicket by its horns became the sacrifice instead of his son Isaac."

"Don't get it."

"Your compass is pointing toward a ram in the bush."

"I need a ram in the bush? Where do I find it?"

"Just stay the course with your compass. As long as you're faithful and keep your eyes open, that's where you'll find your reference letter."

"Can't you make some calls for me?"

I didn't want to tell him I had no one to call. "No time now. Got to get ready for tomorrow."

The next day, it was all hands on deck for the second annual Harlem Ben & Jerry's Street Festival, which filled a closed 125th Street block with kid-friendly games, sidewalk gawkers, tie-dyed T-shirts, speeches by community activists, politicians shaking hands, and lots of free ice cream.

I scanned the large Saturday crowd and saw Ben and Jerry with Anita Roddick, founder of the Body Shop, who had flown in from abroad to celebrate the occasion with them, wading toward me through the throng like the rock stars they named their ice-cream flavors after. Anita located her Harlem store right across 125th street from the Ben & Jerry's, but had the good sense to ignore my petitions and not to hire the homeless to sell her upscale cosmetics.

To my surprise, there was Nate in the midst of the trio, running interference for them, like a pulling guard on a tailback sweep, pausing only to introduce the local councilwoman. Who appointed him to be a celebrity escort?

Nate led Ben and Jerry up onto the platform to their seats. As he brushed by me I whispered, "What are you doing?"

"Using my compass," he whispered, without looking my way, directing Ben's attention to someone else in the crowd.

As Ben spoke about the company's core values of balancing economic, product, and social missions in his passionate but laid-back way, it finally hit me. Nate was standing by the platform waiting for Ben to finish. I flashed him a knowing smile and he discreetly returned it.

Nate had become Ben's self-appointed special assistant for the day to cultivate the reference he needed for the letter, for which he had Ben's commitment before the end of the festivities. I typed it during cleanup, and Ben happily signed before heading back north.

The following Monday, Nate delivered the reference letter. The boss was there—more impressed than ever—and hired Nate on the spot.

At the Harlem Ben & Jerry's party celebrating Nate's new job, I pulled him aside. "How'd you come up with that—Ben for the reference letter?"

"I'd never seen Ben before that day. It was the beard. He looked like a ram in the bush. My ram."

Sharpen Your Tools

Sharpening your *work tool* means building your character and your career, a balanced agenda that is achieved by pursuing both internal and external goals. The quest begins with the understanding that we all have flaws, weaknesses, and shortcomings that can lead to bad choices. Live with integrity: work hard at correcting your flaws, strengthening your weaknesses, rectifying your shortcomings, and structuring a code of behavior for yourself based on your beliefs about right and wrong. In this way you can limit—and even eliminate—bad choices and start making good decisions, which will bring you closer to your career and life goals. The touchstone tools are more about integrity than talent because a little talent with a lot of integrity will go further in life than a lot of talent with little integrity. The following steps will help you build the strength of character that will enable you to be a success at work and at life.

Step one: Work on your character. You are likely inclined to work hardest on your external goals (school, work, hobbies, etc.), while working hard at developing your inner life tends to be an afterthought. You need to make it a priority. There's an old saying in football that the team that makes the fewest turnovers wins. This truth pervades all sports. My fumble becomes a steal in basketball, a double-fault in tennis, an errant throw in baseball, a false start in track. Whatever the sport, bad decisions that lead to mistakes can cost you a win. This principle is also true in life. Your inner journey to integrity is about keeping your turnovers, your self-induced obstacles, to a minimum. The critical point is this: your decisions and choices are not made in a moment in time, but they're rooted in your character. If you have good character, you reflexively make productive choices. If you don't, you risk making bad choices and destroying opportunities. Moreover, having good character will improve your job prospects. Employers are looking not only for skilled people, but for honest, punctual, reliable, hardworking people—people of integrity. Not having as much education, expertise, or skill as the next person may not be a disadvantage if you possess more integrity, because character adds value. Strive for a balance of character and career development—be both talented and trustworthy—and you'll not only be a better person but your job opportunities will abound.

Step two: Work on your capabilities. In biblical times, Jesus was a carpenter; his disciple Peter, a fisherman; the great apostle Paul, a tentmaker. Just as they had the ability to provide something of value in the marketplace of over two thousand years ago, you need to focus on developing your natural talent into a skill relevant in today's economy. Invest in yourself to gain or improve your skill set and upgrade your capabilities, thereby increasing your value to potential employers. Scooping ice cream may not be your dream job—it wasn't for Nate and his coworkers. But sometimes you have to start small in order to get where you want to be. An internship, menial job, or even volunteer work can lead to a flourishing career. Whatever your God-given talent, gift, or ability, cultivate it to its highest level. Whether you use your capability in the business office, the tradesman's shop, the official's household, the athletic arena, the concert hall, or in some form of ministry or community service, work it as though it is a divinely inspired vocation, and keep working at it and learning about it. The key is to cultivate a learning style that's continual because of the ever-shifting twenty-first century job market. In today's globally competitive economy, employers want you to be adaptable, to be ready to plug in and play to dynamic, new environments. That means self-upgrade as you go. Become a lifelong learner.

Step three: Work on your credentials. Capabilities are important, but credentials will be your key to the door of the workforce. Don't get mad at the person who got the job you wanted. Get busy. Get better. Work harder. There'll be another opportunity. Get ready for it. It doesn't matter whether you are white collar, blue collar, or no collar. The decisions—big and small—you make today and every day will greatly influence how socially mobile you are, how self-sufficient you will be, how high up the socioeconomic ladder you will climb.

Your pathway of personal progress will be paved, to a large extent, by your attaining credentials: high school to trade school to community college to four-year college to graduate and/or professional school to on-the-job training to professional certifications to continuing education—the list goes on and on. The further you go on the educational/credential road will fuel your journey toward personal fulfillment, economic success, inspirational living, and divine destiny.

Step four: Work on your code. You should establish a moral code and a firm set of personal convictions—a set of beliefs about right and wrong. For me, the ultimate guide for my personal code is the Bible. I believe the Ten Commandments and other scriptural precepts are rules for my life, so I strive to live in accordance with them. The first thing you must do is check your code; if it includes hating others, killing people, or any kind of evil, it is dead wrong. Get rid of it fast! If you don't have a code, start cultivating one at your home, school, house of worship, even at work. Whether your code is religious or secular, it should create for you not only a system of right and wrong but also regimens of life that challenge you to become a better person. Discover ethical truths in various books—religious texts, the classics of world literature, books about great men and women, books with moral insight and righteous themes. Be clear on the origin and operation of your code and how it plays out in your life day to day. You may not be a religious or spiritual person, but you can still develop a code that helps you to navigate the challenging situations of everyday life; that serves as a guidepost when you're faced with moral dilemmas; that gives you the presence of mind and the strength to stop and consider the rightness or wrongness of an act and to hold to what is right, even when that's very hard to do; and that guides you to make choices that uphold your integrity and serve the best interests of others.

Step five: Work on your compass. Working on yourself is also about cultivating your compass: your moral sensibility, your conscience, that inner voice that knows what is right and wrong—and it cuts across all cultures, religions, and belief systems. While your code comes from the outside, your compass rises from the inside. Use your code to cultivate your compass, disciplining yourself to listen to that voice inside you that guides you in making the right choice, making each experience an opportunity to grow from your decision making into a person of integrity. Compassion is another way to cultivate your conscience—deciding to put the needs of others before your own. Indeed, some of the wisest, most virtuous people in the world are those who have devoted their lives to helping those less fortunate; such people can inspire your own compass. You may feel that working on your moral compass represents moral shackles: rules, restrictions, obligations—things that rein you in and keep you from doing what you want to do. But the irony is that developing your compass is all about keeping your options open—the choice to do right or wrong. Embrace your free will—it's your God-given prerogative. There is power in recognizing that you are ultimately free as a moral agent: when you arrive at a crossroads, you decide to take the high road—or not. What could be more freeing, or empowering, than the knowledge that, in any given situation in which a moral choice is called for . . . it's all up to *you*? When your moral compass is working well, integrity becomes an impulse, a habit of mind. Since repetition is the mother of skill, the impulse to "automatically" do the right thing will kick in like a reflex. When straying from the righteous pathway, your conscience will check you and bring you back in line. You will better be able to ignore temptation, resist peer pressure, and strive for a lifestyle of integrity. More than this, you will begin to radiate your inner light.

WORK AFFIRMATION

I will work harder on myself than on anything else to keep from becoming my own worst enemy.

TOOL #8

WEALTH
THE OPPORTUNITY
BUILDING RESOURCES

A night off at the shelter turned into the all too typical late night at my law workspace. I'd convinced myself that the poorly lit cubbyhole buried at the back of a Harlem office suite was really a place of business, though recollections of the well-appointed Wall Street law firm where I worked as a summer associate mocked my pretensions. What added insult to injury was that this would-be office building was formerly the Hotel Theresa, whose fall from storied bedroom suites to subpar commercial space had foiled my plan to establish a professional Harlem presence in its most famous building as a way to attract clients.

I sighed, looking up beyond the mountains of folders to be filed and gazing at the cracked windowpane and leaky ceiling stains, trying to convince myself that these two cramped, musty rooms were still a better setting for my solo law practice than my brownstone basement apartment.

My stomach growled, distracting me from the motion I was drafting. I'd worked right through dinner again, so I called Harkhomes for help. Though there were many burdens of running that shelter, one of the benefits was the plethora of takeout-fetching volunteers readily willing to bring food for a nice tip.

Tonight it would be Chuckie's turn to be up on the delivery rotation, and as the new kid on the block, this would be his first time picking up for my vegetarian diet, which was not always easy to maintain in a neighborhood populated mostly with greasy spoons and soul food restaurants.

Also, potentially problematic was Chuckie's loquaciousness. He was the intellectual in the current cast of Harkhomes characters—too brash and arrogant for his underperforming lifestyle—ever poised to engage in vigorous discussion, which normally I loved, but I had no time for one with a court appearance looming in the morning.

My mood had soured while working on the documents for the hearing, in which I was representing another slumlord evicting tenants. The contradiction between helping to house the homeless and helping those who were spawning the homeless was excruciating, leaving me with the tortured choice—go broke or go to hell.

Given my hunger pangs, I was pleased by Chuckie's speedy arrival but not with his bloody hand. "Elevator wasn't working," he reported. "I slipped on a loose tile coming up the stairs."

"Sorry about that." I examined the wound, remembering the long-missing bulbs that made the dark stairwell a particular hazard. I searched the office for a bandage, in vain. I sent Chuckie back out with the money to pick up my food plus extra to stop and get Band-Aids.

A native son of Harlem, Chuckie was raised in the Grant Houses, a gargantuan federally sponsored housing project, one of eight in Harlem containing thousands of units apiece. Chuckie had avoided the dependency, low expectations, family disintegration, and gang subculture that many of these monstrosities had fostered. When I asked him how he managed this feat, he proudly proclaimed, "Aunt Betsy!"

Chuckie's aunt lived across the street in Morningside Gardens, a middle-income cooperative that related more to nearby Columbia University than to its stone's-throw Harlem neighbors. A private school English teacher, Aunt Betsy helped her single-mom sister raise Chuckie, forcing the youngster not only to complete all his homework but also to do extra reading, a habit that he retained. I was stumped by the fact that all of his book knowledge had failed to translate into personal initiative.

This much I knew: Chuckie was a twentysomething legend in his own mind, lost in the imaginary worlds of the works of fiction in which he indulged. Unfortunately, he'd rather stick his head in a book than take any initiative like interviewing for a job or reapplying to college (he hadn't yet finished a semester, refusing to work in classes for which he lacked passion). "Actions speak louder than words" was my constant challenge to him. What made him special was that he'd survived the Harlem projects without the baggage—the police record, the substance abuse, the near-illiteracy—that deferred so many dreams.

"Why don't you go to this workshop on jobs emerging in our new information age?" I recently confronted him, passing him the flyer for the free event.

"I'm reading a bestseller about it now," he responded. "My plan is to start my own tech company once I finish it."

Though his ambition was to make a lot of money—"I'll have my first million before I turn thirty," he often promised—he was clueless about how to earn enough to pay rent. He read and talked about his heroes: Jacob Astor, Andrew Carnegie, J. P. Morgan, Henry Ford, even Madam C. J. Walker, his "favorite American tycoon." But turning his pecuniary dreams into practical reality proved to be a particular challenge.

Sow Your Talent

Chuckie returned with provisions. I cleaned then bandaged his injured hand. "Do lawyers make a lot of money?" he asked.

"Some do," I responded, not altogether comfortable in sharing my challenged economic condition. "I don't." I was totally unprepared for his next question.

"If you had worked on Wall Street making a lot of money instead of in Harlem making little money, couldn't you have used all that money to help a lot more homeless?"

I'd been deluged with this kind of question from relatives, Ivy League schoolmates, and professional peers, but now from a Harkhomes resident? My moment's reflection gave him the chance to pontificate.

"Our capitalist system breeds self-gratifying people, and the ambition eats them alive. I want to make a lot of money but I'm afraid, like you, of getting addicted to affluence."

I was about to take another bite of rice and beans but figured any further delay in responding would lead to his usual soapbox of scrambled ideas. Fortunately, I had a well-practiced retort.

"If I had gone to work on Wall Street intent on making money to give to charity, my professional work would have been like the farmer whose seeds fell on the rocky places in Jesus's parable of the sower. Without a deep-rooted commitment in either finance or altruism, the withering of the initiative in the heat of life's vicissitudes would have been inevitable."

"So are you saying going after the big bucks is a bad thing?"

I tried to keep drafting as we talked but I put down my pencil. This next point was too important to multitask through. "You are made in the image of God, the Creator. Your fundamental nature is as a creature of enterprise, engineered to use your God-given abilities to bear fruit from the resources at hand. You were divinely designed to make your own opportunities for wealth, to be self-sufficient, to provide for your immediate needs. Forget the big bucks. Why haven't you been making at least the little bucks?"

"You know the system's not fair, Rev. Stacked against guys like me. If I had an even playing field, I'd be a millionaire by now."

He was confusing capitalism and economic injustice. I considered contrasting the system's entrepreneurial upside with its abuse-of-power downside. But to avoid polemics and keep the spotlight on him,

I resisted a counterpoint and returned to the Word of God. "Do you know the parable Jesus tells about the three talents?"

"One of the three is the farmer planting seed you just mentioned," he stated confidently.

"You need to spend less time reading science fiction and more time reading Scripture." I gently chastised him for confusing the two Biblical accounts.

"Sorry, Rev, you talked about this the other day, right—it's the three guys investing money?"

"Matthew's gospel, the twenty-fifth chapter instead of the thirteenth chapter," I clarified.

"At least I had the right book."

"What about reading fewer comic books and more Bible!"

"I don't like fire and brimstone."

"Start with the New Testament—plenty of love and peace in there."

"Okay," he sighed.

"What else do you remember from the Matthew twenty-five parable?" I encouraged him.

"The third guy messed up the money," he recalled.

"Not exactly." I was pleased that he was moving in the right direction. "Jesus describes a master who gave a portion of his money to each of three of his servants according to their abilities. If the third one—"

"The other two made some money," he interrupted.

"One translation states that the master gave the servants talents, but my favorite version says he gave them bags of gold," I explained.

"I like that version, too!"

"The master gave the first servant five bags of gold, the second servant two bags, and the third servant one bag."

"Why did the master discriminate? Was he white and the third servant black or something?"

"No, there was no discrimination. It was a fair distribution because the master gave to each one according to his ability. And he also gave the servants the opportunity to make money."

"I remember it now," Chuckie enthused. "The first two servants doubled their money, which pleased the master."

"And the third?"

"He lost the bag of gold? Bad investment?"

"He still had the bag," I explained. "But he lost the opportunity. He buried it out of fear. The master was upset and told him, 'You should've put the gold with the bankers so I would have earned some interest on it.'"

"Wow," he uttered. "There were bankers paying interest in Bible times."

"This parable isn't really about money," I quickly clarified, not wanting Chuckie to miss the main point. "It's about your ability to make the most out of the opportunities you're given and the resources you have at hand. Two succeeded because they wisely used what they'd been given. The third failed because of his flawed character. Which guy are you?"

"I see where you're going with this, but I'm not the third guy," he countered.

"Are you using your God-given talent and abilities to the utmost?"

"All I need is the right opportunity and I'll make the most of it."

"You need to figure out how to use your abilities to create a job opportunity right now. You're a smart guy. You need to sow your talent in the fertile ground of college so you can bear some fruit—a good-paying job."

For the first time that night, Chuckie had no fast response. I pressed my point.

"You got my analogy, right?"

Ignoring me, he pulled a dog-eared law school treatise off my antique bookshelf and carefully turned the pages.

I glanced at my watch, realizing how much time I'd lost for my legal work. "Are you listening, Chuckie?" I'd lost my patience. "You need to go back to school or get a job!"

His eyes were still scanning the treatise. "I want to be a lawyer like you."

"Let's talk about it another time." I refocused on the river of papers flowing across my desk. "I've got some lawyering to do right now."

Seize Your Time

"I used to work in an office," he persisted, still perusing the treatise.

Half-listening, I stayed focused on drafting my document.

"Summer job for a couple of years, working in the school office. Aunt Betsy got me in there."

I was torn between the ministry opportunity and my legal work . . . Maybe I could multitask through the conversation . . . It was going to be a long night. "Did you make some money?"

"Not much. Minimum wage. But I showed up to work on time."

"Congratulations." As soon as I said it, I regretted the sarcasm. Now I knew how tired I was.

"Time is money." Chuckie read the framed maxim, one of the only wall hangings in my unadorned office. "Aunt Betsy paid me a little bonus, said I'd earned it because I was never late."

"Time is a valuable resource for everyone," I quickly added, looking up from editing my draft, trying to compensate for my lapse. "But this is especially true for a lawyer because you charge clients by the hour." I couldn't resist the next question, making sure to rectify my tone. "What about you—are you maximizing the value of your time?"

It was a rhetorical question. The expected answer came.

"I read a lot."

"Rereading *Hyperion*, *Dune*, and *1984* are not a wise use of your time. Using time wisely will lead to economic opportunities. Think of it as a resource. You only have twenty-four hours, seven days a week. You must use your time strategically for the productive things, things that will make you money."

"What about reading this?" He held up the treatise.

"What about reenrolling in community college and reading the assignments so you can pass the course?"

He put down the treatise, folded his arms, and stared back at me. Since I had his full attention, I hit him hard with the truth. "You've been wasting time! You need to cultivate this precious resource called time. Then you will be prepared with the right plan to go to school, get a job, make money, move out of Harkhomes, buy your own groceries, and pay rent for your room!"

"Take it easy, Rev," he said defensively. "I'm a young guy. I still got time to get it together."

"Really?! You dropped out of high school."

"I didn't like my teachers, but I went back, got the diploma."

"You started community college but didn't finish the first semester."

"Yeah, but it was a rough time because I'd just broke up with my baby momma. I'm going back."

"You stopped going to your NA workshop."

"That place was just crazy so I'm looking for—"

"Stop the excuses!" My patience was truly wearing thin at this point. "You got talent and you've had time, but now you must seize the moment and make the most of the opportunities that your talent and time afford you. If not, you're going to stay broke!"

Chuckie glared at me. It was a hard blow of truth. He possessed unusual intelligence to have ended up in his tragic and challenged circumstances, but it would be more a curse than a blessing as long as he failed to confront his real problems—his insecurities, substance abuse, laziness, misplaced priorities, and fiscal irresponsibility.

"Got an idea, Rev." He surprised me with this initiative. I'd thought my last rant would've chased him out of there back to Harkhomes.

I finally looked at my watch and gasped. "Let's talk about it tomorrow. I really need to finish my work."

He was unrelenting. "Would I be crazy to say you need some help around here?"

Chuckie ran his fingers across my desk, raising ominous dust clouds. He gently kicked an overflowing trashcan, and some papers spilled to the floor. He grabbed a handful of unopened mail and picked up a stack of papers sitting on top of a stuffed accordion folder marked "TO BE FILED." Then he collected from the floor a stray paper from the motion I was supposed to be drafting and handed it to me.

"Don't you need an assistant?" he asked.

It wasn't an altogether outlandish idea. My part-time secretary had moved on to a better-paying job, so my hands were the only ones on the office deck, and the tide was always rising. "Are you applying for the job?"

"Haven't you been telling me to seize the time?"

His question raised my half-closed eyes.

Before I could respond, he pressed his point. "Working for you can be my opportunity."

I had no time for a job interview, but his initiative compelled me. "What are your qualifications?"

"I can type." He sat down at my antiquated typewriter—no funds yet for one of the new computer-like word processors—inserted a sheet of paper, and pecked away.

"I'm not fast," he confessed, "but steady."

"Where'd you learn to type?"

"My aunt taught me. We had a deal. Whenever I stayed with her, I had to practice typing. Then she'd let me watch *Star Trek*."

"You being a Trekkie is no surprise." We shared a laugh.

"So I can help with your typing, proofread your documents, make copies, do deliveries, clean up, and other stuff that comes up."

His offer sparked an idea for an entrepreneurial opportunity, setting up a real estate brokerage under my law license with Chuckie as my salesperson. He was smart enough to pass the licensing exam, if he'd study for it. With all the bargain-priced, abandoned properties around Harlem those days, this could be a real job for him and an income stream for me. But, as usual, I was rushing ahead into the unknown—better to punt.

"Let me think about all this," I told him. "I'll let you know in a couple days. You are way past curfew. I'll call over to—"

He cut me off. "Let me stay a little while longer to clean up around here. Show you what I can do. A kind of job interview."

Though I wanted to refuse, it was an offer too good to pass by, given the disorder of my office. Besides, I was too tired to put up any more resistance to his determination.

He grabbed an empty manila folder and stuck the first few papers from the "TO BE FILED" stack into the folder. I wondered if this was really a good idea but knew that the train had already left the station.

"Start over there," I instructed him, "with those folders on top of the file cabinet. File them in the cabinet in alphabetical order."

"I got this, Rev," he enthused over his first assignment. "Get your work done. You got any garbage bags?"

I pointed him in the right direction and started writing, but the session with Chuckie had consumed me. It wasn't long before I'd dozed off.

Save Your Treasury

I wasn't sure how long I was napping when Chuckie nudged me. I yawned, rubbing my eyes.

"What do you think?" he asked.

I looked around. I couldn't believe my eyes. The place was immaculate—organized as never before. All my scattered folders had been filed away, books shelved, the floor swept, the trash can emptied, my desktop dusted off—even my pencils sharpened.

"Do I get the job?"

"You're pretty close."

"Pretty close? What do I have to do? Pass a white-glove test?"

"No, but you need to pass the money management test."

"C'mon, Rev," he pleaded. "Stop playing the tough guy. You know I earned this!"

Chuckie had demonstrated his zeal but not his stewardship. He was one of those guys who regularly disappeared on check day. "You want to be wealthy, right?"

"That's why I want this job—to get started."

"Wealth is not just about making money but managing the money you make."

"What you saying, Rev?" He was worried.

"I'm not hiring you if you're going handle my payday like you handle your welfare check day."

"I don't always blow my money."

His cockiness had vanished. This would be a bitter pill for him to swallow, but since he wanted the job so badly, I planned to make him swallow it.

"C'mon, Chuckie, you're talking to Rev, the one who's there waiting for you to show up on check day, but you never do."

"I'll do better," he said diffidently.

"I'm not hiring you to enable your bad money habits."

"I said I'll do better!"

"That's what Nate said—you remember Nate?"

"Of course," he recalled. "He's the Ben & Jerry's guy who came to share his testimony few weeks ago."

"You remember where he is now," I asked him.

"Managing a clothing store. What a testimony!"

"You don't know the whole story."

"Did he stay broke?" Chuckie wondered.

"After he started working at the clothing store," I explained, "a curious pattern developed. He got paid once a week, cash, and every payday, he was late, missing dinner, which had never happened before this. One time he came in after curfew. Another time not at all until the next morning."

"Did he say he was working late?"

"Sometimes that was it, but he always had an excuse: 'My mom got sick and I had to go see her after work'; 'I had to drop off some money to my baby momma's house and I stayed for dinner'; 'I had to work real late and hung around talking to my boss'; 'I treated myself to a movie and lost track of time'; 'I ran into an old friend and he took me out to eat.'"

"I'd be suspicious, too," Chuckie chipped in.

"What really concerned me," I continued, "was that Nate never had any money; all of it would be gone the day after payday. I confronted him with the Word, comparing him to the broke man described by the Old Testament prophet Haggai. '*You earn wages, only to put them in pockets with holes in them,*' I told him, paraphrasing Haggai 1:6.

"Since nothing changed, one payday afternoon, I rounded up three of the Harkhomes residents, and we took the subway downtown to his job around quitting time. As we arrived, another group of four men appeared. We speculated that they were buddies from Nate's former life who knew when he would have money in his pocket, waiting to go drinking and drugging with him."

"Nate must've got the shock of his life," Chuckie said, chuckling.

"He sure did. He came out of the store and looked to the right and saw us and looked to the left and saw them. Then he gave a nervous laugh, shrugged his shoulders, and quickly walked away with his buddies."

"Worst thing he could've done," Chuckie offered.

"No, best thing," I corrected. "He showed his true colors and gave me the license for tough love."

"You laid down the law, huh?"

"Before I let him back in late that night, I gave him a clear choice: turn over his pay to me or lose his bed and his job."

"That wasn't really a choice, Rev." Chuckie laughed.

"I left it up to Nate, and he made the right choice. He agreed to flee the menace of his old buddies, and the three Harkhomes guys who were with him that fateful day became his new posse, enforcing the no-association rule."

"He traded in his Ahabs for his Elijahs," Chuckie recalled the association tool, which really perked me up.

"So every payday, he had a Harkhomes escort until he put the money in my hands," I said. "I held it for him, allocating it as needed according to his budget. He eventually developed the self-restraint and discretion and did the right thing with his check. He saved his money for a few months, then moved into his own room."

"Rev, if you give me this job," Chuckie promised, "I'm good with the Nate plan. Hold my pay, budget it out until I get the money management right."

Amazed that he'd talked himself into a job with me for which I had no description or budget, I was about to discuss wages; with my constrained cash flow I was unsure about how much and when I could pay him. I never had to bring it up.

"And, Rev, don't worry about paying me right now. I can start as your intern, until you see my value. Once you know I'm worth it, that's when the pay will start."

Was he reading my mind?

"Can I start tomorrow?" he insisted. "I want to start making money."

He'd won me over. "Okay, tomorrow. I'm here by ten. Well, maybe not tomorrow. Let's say . . . I'll call you when I get in."

"I'll be ready."

"See you then." I nodded good-bye and quickly refocused on my work.

"One more thing, Rev?"

"What?" I looked up, no longer annoyed at his interruptions.

He pulled a book off my shelf and held it up. "I'm trading in George Orwell for Laurence Tribe."

He plopped down on the couch, opened the constitutional law treatise, and started reading.

"What are you doing? You're way past curfew!"

Without looking up from the book, he declared, "I'm seizing the time!"

I yawned, stretched, rubbed my eyes, and picked up my pencil.

"One final thing, Rev?" He got up from the couch.

"Yes, Chuckie."

He pulled another book off the shelf. It was a well-worn Bible.

"I found this when I was cleaning up. You taught me tonight that making money is important, but there's something more important—creating wealth by using the resources at hand. So while you were napping, I read Matthew twenty-five and Matthew thirteen. The parable of the farmer and the parable of the bags of gold work together. Sowing my talent and time in the good soil of this office, that's what will bear my fruit—true wealth—money that will last. I'm borrowing this book, too."

He laid back down on the couch and started reading the Bible.

I got back to work, but not before taking a second to thank God that my food-delivery request had spawned such a serendipitous outcome.

Inspired, I flowed with the energy through the night to perfect my work.

I looked over at Chuckie—he was fast asleep on the couch, cradling the treatise and the Bible in his arms.

I hadn't pulled an all-nighter since law school. This one turned from distress to delight by dawn.

Sharpen Your Tools

Most modern societies equate creating wealth with making lots and lots of money. However, the *wealth tool* characterizes wealth as more than just material abundance. A truly wealthy person possesses a broad range of resources, encompassing all aspects of life: healthfulness, a sense of belonging, the fulfillment of companionship, a loving family, peace of mind, the joy of destiny's pursuit, a transcendent spirituality. The following steps will help you think through how to use your nonmonetary resources to make money and to manifest things of true value, which bring the kind of satisfaction that money can't buy. If you apply them diligently, along with the other *touchstone* steps in this book, you'll never be broke again because your bank account will get richer, but even more important, *your life* will be richer.

Step one: Sow your talent. God has given you time, talents, and other resources and expects you to be a good steward, which means investing them wisely. You were made a creature of enterprise, created to be productive and fruitful—to increase and multiply. That's God's part. Your part is to work at it . . . and work at it . . . and work at it. If you keep at it, you will bear fruit. If you're not yet sure how to use your gifts and abilities, find some rich soil and sow your talent there. Fertile ground is all around: an internship with a big company or a struggling entrepreneur; a volunteer opportunity at a community-based nonprofit; an online contest; a media competition; a family business in need of creative input. Be innovative. Even be entrepreneurial. The opportunity is there if you look hard enough for it. Think outside the box to plant yourself in a fruitful environment in which you can make some money and from which your abundance can grow.

Step two: Seize your time. An indispensable tool in building financial success is to be a wise steward of your time. You, like everyone else in the world, have twenty-four hours in a day and seven days in a week. What you do with it is your choice. You can make it into a resource by filling it with effort connected to your financial goals, or you can be an idle, unproductive person—couch potatoes beware! Each second of time you squander is an opportunity lost to turn that time into a source of livelihood. Make the most of your time—use it to research jobs and money-making opportunities, to network, to polish your résumé, to learn a new skill, to study so you can ace the test. Wasted time equals lost dollars.

Step three: Save your treasury. The *wealth tool* is about maximizing and managing your money, not by placing it with a Wall Street investment advisor or Main Street banker, but by *you* creatively using the resources at your disposal to meet your needs and fulfill your destiny. The touchstone tools are not a financial management workshop other than to offer this straightforward, timeless advice when it comes to money: *Make it, then save it.* Start with the pennies in your pocket. Instead of buying that lottery ticket, open up a bank account. Forget about the get-rich-quick scheme or the casino slot machine and use the money you just saved toward an investment in your own business, the down payment on a home, or your retirement fund. If you're having trouble saving, let a trustworthy friend or relative hold your earnings until you've developed the habit for yourself. You should also develop a detailed budget that you adhere to so that you know exactly where your money is going and that you are spending responsibly. If you spend wisely and save aggressively, you will be making decisive steps toward your financial security and destiny.

Step four: Shape your treasury. The *wealth tool* is a holistic tool— the whole is greater than the sum of its parts, but each part is important. You will improve your finances as you shape your treasury, using the first three steps of this tool as opportunities to build your wealth. If you sow your talent (which represents the wealth of your God-given gifts and abilities) and you seize your time (which represents the precious commodity of each day as an opportunity for productivity), and if you save your treasury by managing your money once it gets into your hands, you will be shaping your treasury as economic self-sufficiency flows into your life. Don't be single-minded on making as much money as possible. Greed can be a future snare. Be strategic—put your talent and time to work to exploit market information that you've gathered.

And be creative—step into arenas that you haven't tried before. Mine for gold in an unknown stream.

Step five: Share your treasury. "Remember this: *Whoever sows sparingly will also reap sparingly, and whoever sows generously will also reap generously*" (2 Corinthians 9:6). This spiritual principle—about the positive effects of sharing your wealth with others—rises from the physical world. Planting his seed in the ground, the farmer isn't losing his seed but investing that seed in a God-ordained process that will yield a harvest. Giving money away may feel like a loss, but contributing to godly work and worthy causes is really investing with a guaranteed return—"A generous person will prosper; whoever refreshes others will be refreshed" (Proverbs 11:25). So don't get comfortable or complacent once you've made some money and accumulated some savings. Give some of it away. Greater wealth awaits those who are prepared to share abundantly from the full range of resources they possess. "Give, and it will be given to you. A good measure, pressed down, shaken together and running over, will be poured into your lap" (Luke 6:38).

YOUR WEALTH AFFIRMATION

I will find value in talent and in my time; creatively using the full range of my resources; attaining productivity and prosperity; saving, shaping and sharing my treasury.

TOOL #9

LOVE
THE SONG
BUILDING HOLISTIC DEVOTION

I don't feel noways tired
Come too far from where I started from
Nobody tol' me
The road would be easy
I don't believe God brought me this far
To leave me

My rendition of the old Negro spiritual was whispery, since I didn't want to disturb the patient on the other side of the curtain. My singing was for rare occasions, so as not to torment listeners with my off-key melodies. When Big Mike reached for his boom box, I knew it was time to surrender. My Christmas carols had also failed to lift his spirits.

"How'd you like my spiritual?" It was my attempt to reengage him.

"Liked your caroling better. But not much better. Stick to your day job." He turned the volume on his gansta rap back up. I was starting to feel a little depressed. Big Mike's gloominess was infectious.

For almost a week now, Big Mike had been in Harlem Hospital—my least favorite place to be these days. I'd been here a couple weeks ago to visit Tee, and last month for Junior (an extremely painful visit—he was sitting up in his bed one minute; the doctor was pulling the sheet over his head the next).

"Can't you talk to someone here, Rev?" Big Mike implored. "Time to go. I don't want to be here for Christmas."

"I spoke to your doctor the last time I was here. They're not letting go until your blood pressure comes down."

"How come you're the only one who visits me?" He punctuated the question by crunching a mouthful of barbecue chips from the large bag hid underneath the sheets. I knew he was hiding his cigarettes under there, too. I still hadn't figured out how he was smuggling in all this contraband.

I didn't want to tell him that I'd been trying to get others to join me but without success. Big Mike wasn't a Harkhomes favorite because he didn't pull his weight, and he thought he was funnier than he was. His lousy jokes (maybe even worse than mine) had made him kind of a house joke himself. I intended to dodge his query with another Christmas song—never had a chance to.

"What were you talking about the day I fell out?" he reflected pensively. "Something about love?"

He was referring to the morning he collapsed during fellowship—on the floor motionless until the ambulance came. It was a scary moment that happened all too often at Harkhomes. Health crises—though not always this urgent—were a daily challenge.

I was surprised Big Mike recalled the lesson, let alone wanted to discuss it further. He wasn't exactly the exemplary student. Snoozing and joking around were his fellowship meeting pastimes.

"I never had any love," he divulged. This dreary place had a way of making even this sportive big guy solemn.

"I didn't know my dad. Mom gave us up to foster care. Was bounced around from family to family. Juvenile home wasn't home at all."

I hadn't heard his backstory before—it was darker than I expected. Then he went to midnight.

"Never even had a hug from a woman 'til my sister caught up with me couple years ago."

I wasn't sure where to go with this revelation. His pain rose from depths that I could scarcely fathom. I tried Scripture.

"God is love. Whoever lives in love lives in God, and God in them" (1 John 4:16).

"Sounds like Bible stuff," he responded dismissively.

"God's love will show up for you if you—"

"I'm tired, Rev." He rolled over, turning his back to me.

I knew it was time to go.

Love Your Body

I hadn't planned to go back and visit Big Mike the next day, since it was the end of the month and I had to focus on tracking down clients for fees so I could pay rent. As I hurried through the hallway, I tried not to think about the sedated, bandaged young black man rolling by on a stretcher, apparently another gunshot victim up from the emergency room. He looked like one of the teens from the block who came by Harkhomes in search of leftovers to feed his family.

These were precarious times for black men, especially for those at-risk youth whose stories ended—much too often—like the one I just passed. The director of surgery here at Harlem Hospital, Harold Freeman, had recently authored a report that concluded that life expectancy for men in Harlem was shorter than that for men in Bangladesh. I'd viewed the trouble confronting the African American male largely through the lens of homelessness. I knew that the black unemployment rate was more than twice that of white men and that the leading causes of death—homicide, accident, suicide, and close behind, AIDS—were all preventable.

But the Freeman study had now become for me more than simply a set of statistics, more than just a symbol of the dangers of inner-city life. The active threat to the well-being of a thirtysomething black man, living and working in the 'hood, working some of the meanest streets, was made ever more real and personal. I'd never had to confront my own mortality . . . until now. Though I was free of life-threatening illnesses and hadn't been a victim of violent crime, I no longer viewed all the talk about black men being an "endangered species" as paranoid demagoguery. I was but one step away from the next contagion or stray bullet.

Entering his room, I was reminded that Big Mike was plagued by all too common health issues for black men: chronic diabetes, and obesity along with a recent bout with the flu turned pneumonia. Brooding over statistics from the Freeman report, I wondered about poor parenting as the ultimate source of his medical woes. Was he one of those babies born to a mother with lousy pregnancy habits leading to low birth weight? Was he exposed to toxins in overcrowded housing? Subjected to unstable domestic circumstances? I suspected all of the above.

I noticed the beads of sweat permeating his forehead, indicating that his perilously high temperature still hadn't come down. Though it was becoming a long shot with each passing day, I harbored hope that his request would be granted to be released before Christmas Day, which was fast approaching.

I looked around the room for a tissue to mop his brow, but they were nowhere to be found. Formerly a place where African Americans could find decent health care, Harlem Hospital was now plagued by perennial budget shortfalls, equipment breakdowns, medicine shortages, recurrent staff cuts, supply deficits, and in turn, vigorous community protests about substandard care. The good news was that there was always room for my health-challenged guys.

My scurrying awakened Big Mike. "Rev, is that you?" As he rolled over toward me, he inadvertently knocked his half-empty bag of chips to the floor.

"I'll take these." I picked up the chips, seizing the junk food for an illustration.

He opened his eyes. "Sure, you can have a couple."

"You know I don't eat chips. I am taking them from you!"

He was now wide-awake. "C'mon, Rev, barbecue my favorite."

"They're no good for you, Big Mike."

"It's too early for your preaching, Rev. Besides, man, it's just some chips."

"Remember the love commandment we were talking about yesterday?"

"What does that have to do with my chips?"

"It starts with loving yourself," I explained, "but it's not about selfish stuff or ego trips. It's about being a good steward of the person God created you to be."

"Give me an F on that one," he confessed, patting his large belly.

Since I had his attention—a personal application of a spiritual point was a great sign—I wanted to dig deeper into the godly standard of love.

"You have to love yourself holistically." I floated the idea and got the expected response: "Don't get it."

"Think about it this way. You are a three-part being, made up of body, soul, and spirit. Your body is the physical part of you through which the five senses interact with the world."

"Got a lot of that," he guffawed, again massaging his ample midsection.

"Your soul is the mental and emotional part of you, which could be summed up as your personality."

"Got some of that, too," he smirked. "Want to hear another—"

"Save it for the next visit," I cut off his joke, heading for my pivotal point. "Your spirit is the innermost part of you through which you connect with the divine and gain special power to overcome your inner and outer obstacles."

"Sounds kinda deep, Rev," he murmured dismissively. I wasn't letting him off that easy.

"It's really quite simple," I reassured him. "Let's start with the body. You see this bag of chips."

"I want my bag of chips," he said reaching for the bag.

"I know, but hang on a sec. I'm not going to eat your chips. Promise."

"Can I have some while we talk?'

I ignored his request. "God created your body as a holy temple, as a sacred place created in the Lord's image, a beautiful edifice worthy of the best treatment and the highest level of care possible. Your job is to avoid things that defile your bodily temple."

"What's 'defile'?"

"It means to spoil, to degrade, to poison, to ruin, to—"

"I get the point," he cut me off.

"These," I held up the bag of chips, "defile your temple."

"Chips?"

"Chips!"

He looked offended, ready to fire objections, but didn't pull the trigger. It was my sign to keep digging.

"Pass me that Pepsi bottle."

"Can I have the chips back?"

"I'm not done with the illustration."

He reached under the sheets, pulled out the Pepsi, and handed it to me.

"This," I held up the Pepsi bottle, "defiles your temple."

"What do I do?" he threw up his hands in frustration.

"When was the last time you ate a banana?" I pulled one out of my briefcase, hoping it would serve only for illustration, since it was my lunch.

"I don't like bananas."

"What about an apple?" I didn't have one but needed to keep testing the waters.

"Hmmm. Apple. Maybe."

"You like any other fruit?"

"Mango. Used to like mangoes. Been a while."

I thought about stopping there—to give him a break and to try to salvage my regular work schedule. But my penchant for overkill prevailed—I went for the jugular.

"Now hand over the cigarettes."

"Only got a couple left," he resisted.

With great reluctance, he handed them over. "Am I getting this stuff back?"

I ignored his question. "You must refuse to put anything inside your bodily temple that will harm it. Junk food is a no-no. Smoking cigarettes is even worse. Abusing alcohol and drugs worst of all."

"I'm ninety days clean."

"I'm proud of you for that."

"Can I have my chips, cigs, and soda back, then?"

"When was the last time you worked out?"

"What do you think, Rev? Just look at my buffed body."

He laughed and I shook my head as he flopped his flabbiness.

"Loving yourself physically not only means cleaning up the temple but tuning up the fine engine of your body. When you get out of here, you got to get some exercise."

"Don't you see me running the New York Marathon in a few months?" he snickered.

"Walking around the block a couple times a day would be a good start."

"Aren't you late for your meeting?" I knew he was trying to get rid of me; it was time for me to go anyway. I headed for the door, briefcase in one hand, chips, cigarettes and soda in the other.

"Hey, Rev, where you going with my stuff?" he vented.

I kept going, didn't answer, never looked back. From the hallway I heard his voice—"Rev, where you goin', when you comin' back, Rev?" It was tough love to take his stash, but tough love was just what Big Mike needed.

Love Your Soul

So there I was, sitting in Big Mike's room the very next day, unable to resist finishing the tough love lessons.

I got right to the point with Big Mike, pulling out his contraband from yesterday, then juxtaposing an apple and a mango. "Now it's a clear choice: defile your temple"—I pointed to the chips and soda—"or adorn your temple." I nodded at the fruit.

"So Rev, did you hear what happened at the Lenox Ave laundromat last night?" he asked, ignoring the fruit altogether.

I stared at him, bemused that he would just ignore my well-planned presentation to set up what I could tell was one of his jokes.

"Two clothespins held up three shirts." His guffaw filled the room.

I wasn't laughing. On a mission, I didn't have time for jokes, especially not his corny ones.

"Don't worry, Rev." He held up an apple core. "Way ahead of you." There was a tinge of anguish in his voice. Shifting his diet wasn't easy for him.

"Where's the banana peel?" I teased him.

"Don't think it had something to do with what you said," he added. "I overheard two nurses talking about more and more of us dying. They said poor diet was one of the big reasons."

I hid my smile, pleased that the impact of the Freeman report had reached far enough to touch Big Mike.

"You can get rid of the defilement," he waved at the contraband.

He saw the shock in my face. "I told my favorite nurse Naomi about your illustration," he clarified. "She was harder on me than you were. She quoted more Bible at me than you do but she gave me a neck massage when she prayed for me. You never did that." He mocked me with accusatory finger-pointing.

I gleefully dropped the contraband in the trash can, highlighting the breakthrough with a little celebratory dance step.

"Don't start partying yet," he warned. "Y'know I got a stash."

"I'm searching this room before I leave."

"'Fraid of that!" he mocked me this time with a fearful shiver.

"If I find a bag of chips, I'm telling Nurse Naomi."

"You better not." He'd turned serious.

"You're ready for the next step?" I challenged him.

"There's more?"

"Jesus is your role model for the love tool, in word and in deed. The Bible says that Jesus grew in stature—that's the physical. But it also says that He grew in wisdom—that's the mental."

"You got my chips and soda! Now you want my mind, too?"

"Do you really want to get better, or not?"

"You're never satisfied."

"You won't regret it."

"What's next?"

I went to his nightstand and grabbed the pornographic magazine right on top of the stack. "This isn't allowed at Harkhomes."

"I'm not at Harkhomes."

"This is polluting your mind. The love tool is simple. Don't defile your body. Don't pollute your mind." I tossed the porn mag in the trash.

He threw up his hands in frustration. "Gotta pass the time somehow."

I plunged deep into his stack of newspapers and magazines, discovering more pornographic pieces, which I trashed.

"Ouch!" he overreacted each time his X-rated magazines landed in the trash can.

"Can I maybe keep one?" he pleaded.

"One is too many. The Bible says that you can be transformed by the renewing of your mind."

At the very bottom of the pile I pulled out the Bible I'd given him. I melodramatically dusted it off with a mock cough for effect.

"Remember this?"

"You won't let me forget it."

"You tried your best to bury it." I brandished the Bible at him like an angelic warrior wielding the sword of the spirit. "This is your anti-pollution tool. Read a chapter a day. Starting with the New Testament. You got to clean up your mind."

I leaned in to reinforce the point. He'd turned away to ignore my glare.

"Look at me, Big Mike." He grudgingly glanced my way. Our eyes met. "A chapter a day." I turned to the fourth chapter of Philippians. "And memorize this passage: 'Whatever is true, whatever is noble, whatever is right, whatever is pure, whatever is lovely, whatever is admirable—if anything is excellent or praiseworthy—think about such things'" (Philippians 4:8).

He stared at me blankly.

"It is the intensity of your focus on the good things that will renew your mind, breaking it free from its bondage to the bad things." I ripped off a piece of newspaper, marked the page, and handed him the Bible.

"Got a meeting to go to, righ'?"

"You know you can't get rid of me that easily."

"Can't fault a guy for trying."

I went over to his boom box and popped out the cassette.

"Rev, leave my music alone," he threatened.

I held up the cassette tape. "Notorious B.I.G."

"So?"

"Loving your soul means creating the conditions in your mind and emotions that produce wisdom and peace," I expounded. "What you let into your soul is just as important as what you put in your body. Mental self-love is a choice. You must resist the negative thought patterns and embrace the positive ones. Your victory is in your strategy. You'll never figure it out with all this brain clutter."

I looked through the cassette tapes on the nightstand. "Wu-Tang Clan. Tupac. Eazy-E. Snoop. Dre. You got some really inspirational stuff here, don't you?"

"You ol' school, Rev," he protested. "Just because you upset I ain' got no Motown, doesn't give you the right to trash my gangsta rap."

"Wrong. I'm not trashing it, just borrowing it. Let's call it an experiment."

"Anything like your illustration yesterday?"

I pulled a set of cassette tapes out of my briefcase and swept his gangsta rap tapes in. "How'd you guess. It's somewhat analogous. Another negative-for-positive exchange."

I directed his attention to my tape collection. "Here you have sermons from my favorite preachers, and this one is one of my sermons. And I've included the one with praise and worship songs. The key is to fill your mind with inspirational stuff to crowd out your doubts, fears, anxieties, and insecurities—the negative stuff that keeps you from thinking clearly and strategically about your personal progress."

"Not doing it," he shook his head. "I'm not listening to your stuff."

"How are you going to clean up your soul?"

He defiantly folded his arms and looked straight ahead, avoiding my searching eyes. I grabbed a tape from the nightstand and popped it into the boom box.

"I'm not listening." He put his hands over his ears.

"This isn't mine. It's one of yours." I hit "Play." He recognized the beat. Surprised, he slowly took his hands down. "You playing MJ?"

"It's my favorite Michael Jackson song," I told him.

We listened to the lyrics of "Man in the Mirror."

The king of pop's voice rang out: "I'm gonna make a change."

As the song played on, he looked back at me. Our eyes met. "My favorite one, too," he declared.

As the final line of the chorus played, I saw a tear trickle down his cheek. I hoped that he would take the words to heart, taking a look at himself and making a change.

I glanced at my watch—way overtime again. The song ended. I hit the button to rewind. I gave Big Mike a hug. As the song played again, I grabbed my bag and left—with all his mental contraband.

Love Your Neighbor

Even with my frequent forays to these forlorn wards, I'd never been three days in a row, but here I was again the next day, visiting Big Mike.

He was happy to see me, greeting me with a joke. "Hey Rev, what was the favorite rock group of the angels at the empty tomb?"

A Bible-themed joke? Usually I plugged my ears for his humor. What was going on here? "I don't know."

"The Rolling Stones." As we shared a laughed, I thanked God for the miracle: it was not only clean, it was funny.

"Where'd you get that one?" I asked.

"Nurse Naomi. She heard my praise and worship music and got excited. She's an evangelist at her church. She told me her testimony and prayed for me and taught me a praise song that wasn't on your cassette."

"Which one?"

He started singing. I joined him.

What a mighty God we serve
Angels bow before Him
Heaven and earth adore Him
How can you ignore Him
What a mighty God we serve

As soon as we finished the song, he held up an apple core in one hand and a banana peel in the other. "Nurse Naomi told me to go the extra mile."

I saw a booklet on his bed.

"What's the little book?" I asked, pointing to it.

"Nurse Naomi again. She gave it to me last night. Devotional book. Inspirational reading for every day of the month. Playing catch-up. I've already read the first week of December."

"Cleaning up your mind?"

"It's a start."

"I got a surprise for you."

"Rev, you know I don't like surprises."

"Surprise!" I screamed. That was the signal. Six men from Hark-homes filed in. Big Mike was shocked, even more so as each man approached him, giving him a bear hug.

"I got one thing to say," he addressed the group. "Praise the Lord!" he bellowed, in playful mimicry of my teaching style. Everyone laughed—a historic moment, given Big Mike's lousy joke-telling track record. Even I chuckled, having finally gotten over the hypersensitivity of being made the butt of jokes, which still happened much too often.

We made a semicircle around his bed. I leaned in toward him but spoke loud enough for the group to hear. "Big Mike, my time with you the last two days inspired me to share in fellowship last night about love as Jesus commanded it. This moment is about *agape* love: when you love even if your act of love doesn't benefit you in any way. Loving yourself spiritually is all about compassion—loving your neighbor, sacrificing yourself for someone else. Your brothers realized that they were being blessed at Harkhomes for a reason—to bless others. So they decided to come today to show you some love."

Right on cue Lanky, the house supervisor, read a prepared statement. "We, the men of Harkhomes, love you as a brother. We six were chosen as ambassadors to come today to share our love." He opened the Bible and began to read.

If I speak in the tongues of men or of angels, but do not have love, I am only a resounding gong or a clanging cymbal. If I have the gift of prophecy and can fathom all mysteries and all knowledge, and if I have a faith that can move mountains, but do not have love, I am nothing. If I give all I possess to the poor and give over my body to hardship that I may boast, but do not have love, I gain nothing. Love is patient, love is kind. It does not envy, it does not boast, it is not proud. It does not dishonor others, it is not self-seeking, it is not easily angered, it keeps no record of wrongs. Love does not delight in evil but rejoices with the truth. It always protects, always trusts, always hopes, always perseveres . . . And now these three remain: faith, hope and love. But the greatest of these is love. (1 Corinthians 13:1–7,13).

Inspired, Big Mike pulled himself out of bed and joined the circles. We held hands as Lanky prayed for Big Mike, proclaiming at the end, "Lord, please bless Big Mike with a big blessing!" Big Mike said the loudest "Amen!"

"We have a Christmas carol for you. Can we sing it now?" asked Bet, the baritone in the group.

"As long as Rev doesn't sing," Big Mike jested. I laughed the loudest. Bet led us in song.

O come, all ye faithful
Joyful and triumphant
O come ye, O come ye
To Bethlehem
Come and behold him
Born the King of Angels
O come, let us adore Him
O come, let us adore Him
O come, let us adore Him
Christ the Lord

"Nurse Naomi told me about the woman a few doors down who might not make it to Christmas," Big Mike said. "You guys, follow me. Let's spread the love."

We followed as he hobbled down the hallway to Mabel's room. A feeble old lady, she was delighted by our surprise visit. We gathered around her bed and began to sing. She clapped through "*Deck the*

Halls," swayed from side to side with *"Joy to the World,"* and was moved to tears with Bet's stirring solo of the second stanza of *"Silent Night."*

Nurse Naomi came in to join the chorus. Big Mike introduced her with: "She preaches better than the Rev," which encouraged her sermonette about the meaning of Christmas. She proved Big Mike's point with her wonderful conclusion—"Don't worry about going to the store to buy something. Love is the greatest gift of all. And you've given a lot of love today."

Everyone hugged Mabel as we left, with the biggest hug coming to her from Big Mike.

Later that evening, his blood pressure and temperature plummeted, so he was released from the hospital the next day. It was Christmas Eve.

Sharpen Your Tools

The *love tool* is not about romance, how to find a date, or three steps to a happy marriage. It is about agape love: you give expecting nothing in return. This excellence of love happens in two ways: you love yourself holistically, in body, mind, and spirit; and you love others with a spirit of grace and generosity. Follow these steps to build a life where love abounds.

Step one: Be a light. One night at Harkhomes, feeling discouraged, not sure what to say to a dejected resident, I shrugged my shoulders. He responded: "Don' worry, Rev. You just being here for me is enough." Sometimes just being present is sufficient for the moment. Show up for someone in need. Give a hug. Refrain from indiscretion. Forgive an old hurt. Sacrifice your seat on a crowded bus or train. Point the way to the lost. Throw a lonely starfish back into the sea. Share a moment of silent grief. Brighten someone's day with a smile. A small gesture can be what's needed to make a big difference. Remember—it is better to light a candle than to curse the darkness.

Step two: Be a soldier. Life is a fight for territory. If you don't fight for light, darkness will take over. If you don't fight for truth, falsehood will govern your soul. If you don't fight for inspiration, discouragement will conquer your heart. If you don't fight for vigor, fatigue will rule your body. You can't be a soldier for the right things if you're consumed with the wrong things. Learn not to burn up your energy in stress and worry. Avoid vices like junk food, cigarettes, and drugs, which devitalize you. Being a spiritual soldier demands that you get in shape. Generate more stamina, more energy, more positivity to pass on. Exercise several times a week. Improve your diet with nutritious foods. Your battlefield for self-improvement is ever before you. Be fit and vigorous enough to fight the good fight of personal progress and to struggle on behalf of a worthy ideal.

Step three: Be a sage. To love someone is to help that person see and work toward becoming the best possible version of him- or herself. An overweight, high-fever Big Mike in a hospital bed was not his best version. To start building the best version of you, you must use wisdom in regulating your mental and emotional traffic. Don't let the media you watch, read, and listen to draw you away from information that will edify and inspire you. What you allow into your mind impacts your emotions, stability, and consistency. Immerse yourself in new and enlightening information, stirring fresh reflections to chase away your distractedness over things that are really outside of your control anyway. Memorize Biblical passages, poetry, famous quotations, speeches, and other inspirational sayings. Share these statements with others to reinforce them in your own mind. The wisdom and inspiration you find can spawn life-changing insight to shape that better version of you.

Step four: Be a game-changer. Turn the tables. Change the conversation. Shift the mood. Create an edge. Be the X factor. The goal of this book is to help you build a spiritual, values-based framework into your life; use your newfound strength to become a compassionate builder for others. Do be there for the crisis, to put out the fire. But make sure you're there for the long haul, as the house is being restored, as the pieces of the individual life are being put back together. It may take a while as well as blood, sweat, and tears. But don't just be a fire-fighter. Stay around. Be a builder, bolstering others through their struggles. Share an inspirational saying, a Bible, this book, or some other uplifting work. Pray—sometimes it's your best and only option. It just might change the game.

Step five: Be a gift. Don't give someone something as the gift. Give yourself as the gift. Loving yourself spiritually means giving yourself away, to lift someone who is struggling, to see every day as an opportunity to make a difference in another's life. Don't just pay for someone's lunch; pay for their training workshop so next year the person can pay for *your* lunch. And remember, grassroots engagement is just as valuable as monetary support. So go beyond the handout to touch another with your time and energy. Volunteer at the soup kitchen; pray at your neighbor's hospital bed; fulfill a school or work requirement of community service. Give sacrificially. What if Jesus had thought about the challenge before him and decided, "I don't do crosses." Don't be someone's worst nightmare. Be the answer to someone's prayer.

YOUR LOVE AFFIRMATION

I will love myself as Jesus loved Himself, holistically: loving my body through diet and exercise; loving my soul through inspirational reading and heartfelt praying; and loving my neighbor through compassionate service.

TOOL #10

FAITH
THE NET
BUILDING INNER STRENGTH

"Ray needs a miracle!" Slacky shouted, sparking collective laughter. Ray and I were the only ones not amused.

Another one of my great ideas had backfired. Ray had earned the dubious distinction of having won the Revolving Door Award the most times—this was his eighth Harkhomes tour of duty. I'd established this recognition as a disincentive: to keep men from getting stuck in the revolving door, they were ironically recognized upon each and every return. But with the jeers acknowledging Ray's long and winding road of recidivism reaching this milestone, I felt like I was blaming the victim as Ray the Laughingstock hung his head in shame.

I discreetly studied him, discerning the first chink in the armor of his usually imperious demeanor. There was some truth in Slacky's ribbing. It seemed some kind of supernatural intervention would be necessary to shift the odds so heavily stacked against Ray, but I decided it was best to shift the focus.

"Ray needs a miracle?" I intervened. "You all need a miracle." I exploited the moment with a pop quiz. "Who remembers the question from yesterday's fellowship teaching about miracles?"

Only one hand went up—the expected hand, Church Boy, so nicknamed because he'd retained his florid Sunday-morning demeanor despite his drifting from his religious roots. His rebellious streak had led him to wrong people, places, and things from which he was trying to recover. I could see his faith getting stronger day by day.

"Anybody but Church Boy?" I pleaded, trying to conceal my frustration at the never-failing disinterest of my audience. I nodded at Church Boy.

"Where's your net?" he declared in his southern drawl, recalling my challenging question that concluded the recent session. I'd used a familiar passage—Jesus's calling of his first disciples—for my lesson on faith. Peter and his fellow fishermen had worked all night without a catch, so they were obviously baffled by Jesus's directive: "Put out into deep water, and let down the nets for a catch" (Luke 5:4). Though it made no sense, they believed and put out their nets, and their faith led to a miraculous catch of fish—more than their nets could hold.

"Where's your net?" I'd confronted them. "Is it in the boat? Or is it in the water? If it's in the boat, you're not going to catch any fish."

"Make it plain, Preacher," Church Boy encouraged me.

I drove the point home. "Is your net still stuck on the shores of your unbelief, or have you cast it into the depths of your faith, where your miracle happens? Have the faith to go forth into the unknown. If you stay in the boat on the shore, it means you're a prisoner to your doubt and you won't catch your miracle."

Since all but Church Boy had failed to respond to my question, I decided to keep going until I got through to them. "I'm going to give you guys a chance to redeem yourselves this morning. Now, who can tell me my principle of the week?"

Church Boy's hand shot up. I ignored it, looking around the room at the blank and turned-away faces. "Go ahead, Church—" I caught myself, glimpsing Ray's hand slipping up, which was somewhat miraculous itself, since this was only the second time in countless sessions he'd volunteered a comment. His long-ago question had launched my quest for tools, but an effective implement for him had proven so elusive. I put up one hand as a stop sign for Church Boy and pointed a green light at Ray.

"It's better to do one Bible lesson than to hear a thousand of them," Ray asserted.

"Praise the Lord." I concluded the morning's fellowship, leading an ovation for Church Boy and Ray. Though I couldn't read Ray's poker face, I discerned a positive vibe—or was it just another trickle from my endless stream of wishful thinking?

Build Your Net

Ray avoided me all day, knowing I'd summon him to the office, which I eventually did.

"I'm proud of you, the way you came up with the principle this morning," I encouraged him.

"Thanks, Rev, but I'm helping cook dinner," he parried, "so I don't have time for any questions."

Ignoring his ploy, I got right to the point. "Where's your net, Ray?"

"I don't really believe in anything."

"Yes, you do. You're just not in touch with it. Everybody possesses a belief system, a worldview, a set of convictions or guiding philosophy. Let's consider six types of such people: the devout, the fatalist, the astrologist, the egoist, the atheist, and the pragmatist."

"Rev," he protested, "haven't I heard this before? I got stuff to do."

"This is new material, and there's nothing more important than for you to hear this. Unless you want to head out that front door and start thinking about adding to your world record." It was a hollow threat; I'd never evicted a resident for refusing to listen to one of my pontifications. But the ultimatum was enough to keep him in his seat—at least for the moment.

"The devout is the religious person, someone whose worldview stems from a sacred book like the Bible, the Koran, or the Torah. Such a person believes that ultimate control is held and exercised by a supernatural, omnipotent being. You know anybody like that?"

"You," he said disdainfully. "You're the only monk I know."

It wasn't the first time I'd been accused of being an extremist when it came to my religious devotion. I knew it was his way of rejecting me as a fanatic. I'd learned to take Jesus's approach to such slights—to turn the other cheek and keep going.

"The fatalist has the attitude 'What will be, will be.' Such a person yields all control over what happens to the circumstances, impersonal forces outside of himself. Is that you?"

"Maybe."

"The egoist is a self-centered person, seeing all things revolving around him. Such a person believes that he has total control of circumstances, other people, and the forces of the universe—the master of his own destiny."

"Now that's *really* you, Rev," he insisted, showing enthusiasm for the first time in the discussion. If reviling me was the means of engaging him, I'd suffer through it.

"The pragmatist emphasizes practical results over ethereal realities. Such a person seeks to master all things within his control but accepts the reality of things outside his control. In my worldview, I seek to balance the approach of the devout with that of the pragmatist by living according to this rule of thumb: live as if everything depends on me; believe as if everything depends on God. Faith and works as a daily discipline is an equilibrium I strive to maintain."

"How come I only see the God stuff?"

About to lose my temper over his deepening resistance, I took a deep breath, rubbed my face with my hands, and rushed to the end of my fruitless exercise.

"The atheist disbelieves in the supernatural and the astrologist believes that heavenly bodies influence human affairs. Now, what do you believe?"

"Mom was an astrologist. Dad was an atheist. So sometimes I believe in the stars and sometimes I believe in nothing."

"You believe in Harkhomes."

"Got nowhere else to go."

"You keep coming back. Means you haven't given up. Means you have hope. Means you believe in the possibilities that this place offers you."

"Are we done here?"

I glared at him in anger. He returned defiance. I was feeling absolute futility, and in that moment, Church Boy approached.

"'Scuse me, fellas, sorry to interrupt, but I was praying for you, Ray." He pulled up a chair and sat, leaning in close to Ray. "Just now the Lord gave me a word for you. You're tired. Hard times worn you out. So much adversity, you're exhausted."

"Do I have to listen to this, Rev?" Ray complained. "Like I need more bad news."

"No, no," Church Boy explained, "it's good news."

"Good news that I'm exhausted?"

"It's like this: I was a good swimmer so one summer growing up I worked as a lifeguard on the beach. One day I saw a guy in trouble in the ocean, swam out to him, and immediately grabbed him."

Church Boy's gesticulations enlivened the story. I glanced at Ray, who was much more engaged than during my mini-lecture.

"His thrashing and kicking took us both down." Church Boy hit the floor to dramatize the point. "I had to let go. Good thing there was another lifeguard on duty, who swam out and treaded water nearby, waiting 'til the drowning guy was at the end of his strength; the thrashing stopped, then he rescued him."

"I don't swim, never been to the beach and I don't care!" Ray stood up to go. Church Boy stood, blocking his way. I remained a transfixed spectator.

"Listen, listen, this is the Lord's word for you. You're the struggling swimmer, thrashing around, about to take Rev and others trying to help you down, or scaring them away. You know you're going under, but you still keep doing things the same old way. Stop trying to save yourself so your rescue can begin. Stop all the kicking and screaming. The Lord's arm is but a length away. If you reach out to Him, the Lord will pull you safely to shore."

I was surprised that Ray didn't bolt. He just stood there, grimacing, looking askance, shaking his head.

Impassioned, Church Boy leaned in, almost nose-to-nose. "Remember this—something my father shared with me—'Fear knocked at the door. Faith answered. No one was there.'"

"I ain't scared of nothing."

Though this time Ray walked swiftly away, it'd become clear from the increasingly pained expression on his face as he listened to Church Boy's prophetic utterances that he got the message. I shook Church Boy's hand and thanked him for his boldness. I also thanked God for finding an effective medium for some soul-stirring truths that just may have gotten through to Mr. Revolving Door.

Believe in Miracles

On duty that night, I was endeavoring to finish a real estate contract while monitoring the activities. It was a quiet Saturday night, so multitasking like this should've been less challenging than usual, but I was completely distracted by Ray's hope—the hint of aspiration in his eyes during Church Boy's intrepid intervention.

A phrase came back to me from my college English class: *deus ex machina*. Originating from ancient Greek and Roman dramas, this artistic device denotes a sudden, unexpected, divine intervention that serves as a previously unimaginable solution to an apparently unsolvable problem. It was popularized by Shakespeare in plays like *Macbeth* and used by other great writers as well.

I'd spent much of the evening massaging this idea to articulate miracle-working faith—the sense that, at the last minute, the situation can change completely, fate can be turned around, and opportunity can be created out of despair. But would this concept engage Ray? Probably not, but I had nothing else.

I got up from the office desk to make my rounds. I found Ray in the kitchen, alone washing the dishes. I picked up the dish towel and started drying them. He didn't acknowledge my presence. An awkward minute or two passed. *Now or never*, I thought as the stack of dirty dishes dwindled. About to float *deus ex machina*, Ray surprised me with a question.

"I've heard you talk about your favorite Scriptures. What's your favorite miracle?"

I wasn't ready for his curveball, but I quickly trashed my literary gem and shared some personal gold from long ago. "It's my Aunt Marie miracle."

"Who's Aunt Marie?" I noticed a pause in his dishwashing rhythm. I put down the cloth and told him the story.

The summer after my second year at Harvard Law School I worked at a Washington, DC, law firm. I lived with a close family friend whom I knew as absentminded Aunt Marie. I'd been saving money for a top-of-the-line stereo system to take back with me to Cambridge. When I finally had enough money, I'd withdrawn the twelve hundred dollars from the bank only to find out at the store that my model was out of stock. It was a Friday afternoon and the bank had closed. I hid the money in my room at Aunt Marie's house, intending to buy the stereo the following Monday.

What I didn't know—because she forgot to tell me—was that Aunt Marie was having some rooms painted the next day. When I returned home Saturday evening, I'd found the furniture rearranged and covered, my room painted, and the painters come and gone. My money was missing!

I searched for it in vain. I felt like an idiot. I was angrier with myself than with the painters, for being so stupid to leave that much cash unsecured. I told Aunt Marie, who called me irresponsible, chided me for accusing her painters, and summarily dismissed my concerns. I searched again, never found the money, and chalked it up as a very tough life lesson.

Eighteen months later, after I had graduated from Harvard and was living in Harlem, I was trying to find a legal job in Harlem and having financial struggles—that first year on my own it was hard to keep the wolf from the door with just the freelance legal work I was doing, and all the other demands on my time.

My roommate, James O'Neal, was on a public-interest law fellowship that had not yet been funded. After a few months, all our savings were gone. We were completely tapped out. Broke. And our parents—not thrilled with our "Harlem decision"—were not about to bail us out with a loan.

It was at the point where we didn't even know how we were going to pay that month's rent, buy food, or meet any expenses. James and I just literally emptied our pockets on the kitchen table and counted all the bills *and* coins; it was less than eighty dollars between us. We had no one to turn to, nothing to do but pray.

Suddenly, the phone rang. It was Aunt Marie calling from Washington. Had I, she asked, left some money behind at her house the previous summer? Speechless, I listened as she explained that she'd found a sum of money tucked inside a blouse. The blouse—one of her favorites—was among several that she had removed and put to the side before the painters started their work to preclude blemishing. She was reorganizing her wardrobe, rediscovered the misplaced blouse, picked it up and the cash fell out.

Dumbfounded, I said that, yes, I had left $1,200, but that I'd thought it had been stolen. She told me that was exactly how much money she'd found—and that she was express-mailing me a check in that amount immediately.

"The missing money had become my blessing in disguise," I told Ray. "What had seemed like bad luck at the time had actually been God's handiwork. Providence had prevented me from spending money on a stereo I didn't need to preserve it for a more important future purpose that I didn't know I had—manna from heaven to survive in Harlem. Four months rent that I didn't have was now on the way."

Ray had stopped washing about halfway through my anecdote, listening intently. At the end of my story, I decided to challenge him.

"Do you have the faith for God's creative purpose to work in your own life?"

He didn't say anything, avoiding my glare and went back to washing dishes. I resisted the temptation of further inquiry and did my rounds.

Later, stretched out on my hallway cot, about to close my eyes after another long Harkhomes day, I heard voices from the Fellowship Room. Disgusted, I got up—what punishment would I have to mete out for talking after lights out?

Entering the room, I was arrested by the sight of Church Boy sitting on the floor next to Ray's cot, talking to him. In the surrealism of the scene, I eavesdropped, wanting to partake but also to stay invisible.

Church Boy directed the flashlight and Ray's attention to an open Bible. Church Boy encouraged him to read. I tiptoed closer, leaning in to hear the conversation.

"This is what Jesus said to them," Church Boy whispered, pointing at the Bible. "Go ahead, read it."

"Because you have so little faith," Ray read. "Truly I tell you, if you have faith as small as a mustard seed, you can say to this mountain, 'Move from here to there,' and it will move. Nothing will be impossible for you" (Matthew 17:20).

"Now, let me show this other one," Church Boy effused, flipping the pages to Ray's full attention.

I marveled at the moment. It was unfathomable to me that Church Boy had captivated the impenetrable Ray with a midnight Bible study. I slipped away, resolving that my highest purpose in that night's divine handiwork was to stay out of God's way.

◆　◆　◆

"Rev, Rev, wake up."

Rubbing my eyes, I feared the worst. Whenever I was awoken in the middle of the night at Harkhomes, I expected strife, illness, violence or even death, all of which were true-to-life nightmares I'd experienced.

I opened my eyes to Church Boy's "Good news, Rev." I thought I was dreaming. "I invited Ray to church and he agreed to come." Now I truly thought I was dreaming.

"How'd you get him to agree to church?" I asked Church Boy. "I've been trying forever."

"I told him, 'It's time for you to cast your net out into the deep waters. You will catch something big.'"

"Hallelujah!" I exclaimed, praising God for the breakthrough.

"It also could have been Ray thinking," Church Boy explained, "that the only way to get me to shut up so he could get some sleep was to agree to come to church with me."

"I'll take it. Whatever works." We laughed heartily.

Church attendance for the Harkhomes guys was encouraged but optional. Ray had always opted out. So it was indeed a victory that Sunday morning as he sat in the pew of the nearby Bethel Gospel Assembly—my favorite heathen finally inside God's house. Church Boy and I had stayed up into the wee hours praying for something miraculous to happen to Ray.

But nothing happened. Through the singing, welcoming, dancing, and preaching, Ray sat between Church Boy and me—impassive, slumped. He refused to stand for the reading of the Word, hold hands for collective prayer, march with the congregation during the offering, obviously the only rebellious one in the entire sanctuary. "Is there something wrong?" I probed a couple of times, to no response.

Bishop Ezra Williams preached about forgiveness. He quoted the parable of the unmerciful servant, one of my favorites—"Shouldn't you have had mercy on your fellow servant just as I had on you?" (Matthew 18:33) and exhorted: "Everyone has experienced hurt at the hands of another. It may be the no-show father, the abusive mother, the adulterous spouse, the backstabbing friend, the brownnosing coworker, the ungrateful child. It may be the hardest thing you'll ever do, but you must confess any ill feeling and forgive them so that God can forgive and bless you."

Leaving the church after service, Ray was reticent, nervous, looking around. As he, Church Boy, and I crossed the street into Marcus Garvey Park, he picked up the pace. "Can we walk a little faster?"

"What's wrong?" I asked.

We didn't have to wait long for an answer to Ray's anxiety. A big, middle-aged black man ran us down and introduced himself as Buster. When he'd stood with the other visitors being introduced during the church service, I had a sense I'd seen him before.

"Is there something wrong?" I asked.

Buster pointed at Ray. "He ripped off and raped my sister."

"This guy's crazy," Ray trembled. "Let's go." He tried to flee, but I grabbed one arm, Church Boy the other.

"Don't play with me, Ray," Buster said. "Why don't you tell the truth for once? That's why I'm standing here right now—to tell the truth. My plan was to kill you for what you did to Sis. That's what I used to do for a living. Made big money for my hits. But with you it was personal. I couldn't wait to take you out.

"But you don't have to worry about me now," Buster continued. "I gave my heart to the Lord and I'm doing my best to live for God these days. I heard His message. I need a lot of forgiveness for the life I lived. So I came out to confess my sin toward you and ask you to forgive me for hating you, for intending to kill you, so the Lord will forgive me and continue to bless me."

"Buster!" A voice rang out from the sidewalk.

"Coming!" Buster yelled back. "That's my ride. I got to go. One last thing you need to know, Ray. I don't know who these brothers are, but you got someone praying for you. One night I followed you and was waiting down the block, across the street from some shelter where you were staying. You turned into the block and I had you lined up, ready to pull the trigger. But out of nowhere there was someone walking beside you, right in my line of fire. I couldn't shoot, so I came out from behind the car to change my angle. You saw me with the gun and ran into that shelter. I never got a shot off."

Stunned, I recalled the very moment Ray rushed into Harkhomes, terror in his eyes.

"Buster, we're leaving now!" came the same voice from the street.

As he hustled off, he shouted back, "Pray for me!"

Ray's knees had buckled during Buster's murderous confession, and now he was crumpled on the ground. We dragged him over to a park bench. He was sobbing uncontrollably. "There was no one there," he whimpered. "There was no one there."

I was still fathoming what just happened, but Church Boy proclaimed it. "That was Gabriel walking beside you," he exclaimed. "That was your miracle! The Lord sent an angel to safeguard you. That's who Buster saw. That's why he didn't shoot. The Lord delivered you from the hit man's bullet!"

I joined in the triumphant bear hug on that park bench, marveling at the miracle that Ray disbelieved had already been exercised on his behalf, with today's act of faith bringing him into its awareness. Not usually one to show much emotion, tears of joy flowed down my cheeks as well.

The wonder of the circumstance, with its mysterious intersection of providential power and human predicament, left the three of us sitting there in silent awe.

We were there the rest of the afternoon, listening to Ray confess his legion of sins. He described his life of fear, believing a hitman's bullet awaited him behind every parked car. He acknowledged that a miracle had saved his life, and thanked God for it. Led in prayer by Church Boy, Ray cried out, "Lord Jesus, I place my life in Your hands!"

Before we left the park bench, Ray reflected on the special moment. "Y'know, Rev, when I first came you started talking about these crazy tools but over the years nothing ever worked for me. Now that I know how to use the net, I'm using it all the time."

It'd been a long time coming for Ray to reach his turning point, and for me to grasp the power of the tools. I now knew that the houses of progress that he and Chuckie, Slim, Lincoln, Sandi, and others were building for themselves would not only withstand the storms of life but would also be lighthouses for others. Their toolboxes were full—and so was mine.

Sharpen Your Tools

In our increasingly secular age, faith and religion are unfashionable in a lot of circles and unacceptable to a growing number of people. God is not in vogue. Over the past half-century, Christian churches in America—Protestant and Catholic alike—have been hemorrhaging members, money, and influence. Heretical expressions of traditional Christianity as well as New Age–isms have been proliferating. Consequently, for many, it's difficult to acknowledge that religious beliefs have practical consequences. But amazing, inexplicable, miraculous things still happen by, through and for men and women of strong and certain faith. By writing about religious terms like *miracle*, *Providence*, *divine*, and *faith*, I'm not promoting a particular creed, theology, or doctrine.

Though there may be a lot of religious material in it, this is not a religious book per se. It is about principles and values, not theology or dogma. Though I am a Christian with a firm belief in the supremacy of God, the deity of Christ, and the inerrancy of the Bible, my purpose is not to preach or proselytize but to inspire you based on transcendent truths to strive for the higher ground of personal fulfillment and divine destiny. But you can't get there without faith. Faith is the force that produces the miraculous in our lives. The *faith tool* is a practical principle with supernatural implications; it involves both a dynamic process and a deeper reality. It will help you navigate an inner journey where you will make important discoveries about your own strengths and resources—but also acknowledge that you don't possess all the keys, that doors do open as a result of a power at work in the universe beyond your control that can affect the way things unfold in unexpected, surprising, and yes, mysterious ways. The following steps are to help you get in touch with your faith or to experience it in new, inspirational, and miraculous ways.

Step one: Discover the divine. Launch your inner journey to faith today. The more seriously you take this journey, the greater the possibility you will delve deeply enough inside to discover the divine. God is there. If you haven't found Him yet, it means you haven't looked hard enough or you've been looking in the wrong places. You will unearth God as you dig into your most deeply held values that shape your view of the world, seeking to bring light to those areas that you have longed to understand. Don't settle for what you've been told or taught. Keep digging. Try praying. Ask God to reveal Himself to you. Endeavor to accept that some mysteries of faith, like the divinity and humanity of Christ, are beyond perfect understanding. You may find God in the sanctity of a house of worship or in the solitude of your bedroom. Be intentional about your search. As Jesus said: "Ask, and it shall be given to you; seek and you will find; knock and the door will be opened to you" (Matthew 7:7).

Step two: Determine your beliefs. If you are a religious person, you may find that some of the precepts and experiences described in this book resound in your worship, devotional experience, or lifestyle. If you're not a religious person, you may discover some relevance in the spirituality of this chapter and the book generally as it seeks to help you develop an introspective, philosophical, and serene approach to life's challenges. Knowing what you believe is a critical step on your faith journey. If you're not sure about your beliefs, you need to get in touch with this dimension of yourself by exploring what might be some challenging questions:

Which type of person am I most like: the devout, the fatalist, the astrologist, the egoist, the atheist, or the pragmatist? Or some combination of these types? Or am I most like some other type?

What is my worldview or belief system? What are my deepest convictions? Why do I believe them? Are they furthering or frustrating my personal progress? How is my worldview influencing my lifestyle?

Do I believe in miracles? If not, why not? Have I ever experienced a miracle or known someone who has? Is my faith deep and strong enough to allow a miracle to happen in my life?

As you honestly answer these questions and move along your inner journey toward faith, you just might discover the missing dynamic in the design of your destiny.

Step three: Deploy divine technology. Your smartphone is indeed a miracle of modern technology, but don't miss the reality of divine technology that has been around a lot longer. Distinct from the elements of this world that you can experience through your five senses, the kingdom of heaven is a spiritual system by which God governs the workings of His creation. The godly system can only be experienced through faith. Though you can't fully comprehend them, the rules and laws of God's kingdom operate all the time. If you're living in harmony with these spiritual precepts, this divine paradigm is designed to bless you. If you're living in violation of its laws, this supernatural arrangement is structured to penalize you. Your challenge is to line up your thoughts and conduct exactly in accordance with this kingdom technology so that your observance of godly principles can release grace and favor into your life. An example of the kingdom of God at work in everyday circumstances is the faithful prayer: "Whatever you ask for in prayer, believe that you have received it, and it will be yours" (Mark 11:24). It takes a lot of faith to cast your net in the deep water. Go for it. It will lead you to outcomes that are better—and more fun—than playing games on your smartphone.

Step four: Discern your blessings in disguise. Life has a way of resisting your control, of defying predictability, of introducing unfavorable circumstances, of upsetting your best-laid plans. This doesn't mean you should live with a sense of frustration and futility but with the awareness that the constants in life are challenge and change. If you don't believe so, you run the risk of missing or dismissing the providential interventions that could pop up along the pathways of your life. Be a person of faith—then you will find a purpose in opposition, a silver lining in the clouds, calm in uncertainty, and an opportunity for serendipity in the midst of life's storms. Your faithfulness brings the revelation that when things are at their darkest, good can still prevail. Through it all, you will be able to discern life's adversities as blessings in disguise.

Step five: Dare to believe. Popular culture has turned "Ya gotta believe!" from spiritual affirmation to hackneyed phrase: the clarion call of any long-shot sports team or ailing politician in need of a comeback. Yet its truth remains. Some label it as chance, or coincidence, or good luck, or attribute it to a vague, touchy-feely approach to life in which you do nothing and simply trust that the universe will "make it happen." Believe me, faith doesn't happen that way. "Ya gotta believe" is code for strong faith, the rallying cry for all those who face seemingly insurmountable obstacles—the challenge appears to be impossible to handle, yet somehow, you keep believing and believing, and a way appears out of no way. Faith and miracles are mutually supportive phenomena: the more faith you possess, the more miracles you'll experience; the more miracles you manifest, the more faith you'll have. So when you come to the end of your energy, knowledge, and strength—when you're pushed to the limit and don't know which direction to take, and are about to throw up your hands and admit defeat—all there is left for you to do is to believe. Yes, it's abstract. Yes, it's metaphysical. Yes, it may seem irrational. But for those who believe, guess what? It works! No matter how trying your circumstances, how far away the destination, how high the mountain to climb, dare to believe that you will surmount . . . and you hold on, and help comes at an unexpected time in an unexpected way. When you make your faith strong, the odds shift in your favor. It's as though God responds to your belief in Him, by believing in you.

FAITH AFFIRMATION

I will cast my net of faith and believe in my miraculous catch. I will do everything in my power to move beyond whatever stormy circumstances confront me. Where I fall short, I will believe that God will show up in the midst of it all to take me the rest of the way.

CONCLUSION
WHAT'S IN YOUR TOOLBOX?

What lies behind us and what lies before us are tiny matters compared to what lies within us.

—*Ralph Waldo Emerson*

Life is more than a means to an end. Fulfillment comes from following and achieving one's dreams and the satisfaction of personal growth, no matter what our origins or circumstances. We all seek meaning and connection and struggle with being and becoming the versions of ourselves of which we can be most proud. That is the very point of this journey called life. And nowhere was that lesson made more clear to me than in my life-changing work with the men at Harkhomes.

Providing the shelter, food, and clothing for the men there proved to be the relatively easy part. It was all the nonmaterial sustenance—counseling the residents, helping them figure out how to put their lives back together, researching the housing and job options, being that shoulder to lean on after the endless rejections, fathoming the anger, resistance and depression, praying when all else failed—that yielded the tools, which forged the change in them and me.

I learned that the victory of an inspired life happens beyond the "three hots and a cot." The marvel of personal transformation rises from that inner place beneath the symptoms and the senses, within the soul and the spirit, where the unique potentiality of the individual must be cultivated. Enter the touchstone tools.

The ten tools evolved from slowly building on moral and spiritual accomplishments. The inner journeys that they represent are a never-ending road. Every day represents a work in progress. Each experience is an opportunity to build strength of character. You are constantly faced with choices—moral, practical, and otherwise; the toolbox is designed to help you make the right ones.

As you search for meaning and value in a chaotic, shallow, stressful, cynical world, the tools pave the way for that inward trek where career pursuit is balanced with character development; where spiritual objectives leaven material goals; where what you're becoming on the inside is ultimately more important than what you're achieving on the outside. Shift your focus from the external objectives (higher salary, better job, bigger house, high-flying lifestyle) to the inner goals (being more persistent, more joyful, more visionary, more disciplined, more giving)—which will also move you toward attaining your material goals, but with greater satisfaction. The tools seek to transform you from a life fraught with stormy crises and unfulfilled potential to a life full of self-awareness, personal development, and daily victory.

The tools go beyond personal progress to societal uplift. The dark cloud of national decline pervades in no small part because of the waning of moral values in the American ethos. American malaise stems from a society adrift from the pursuit of individual virtue as a foundation for the collective good. One consequence is the troubling rise in single parenthood across all ethnic groups, signifying a breakdown in virtues like personal responsibility, perspective for the future and relationship-building—important tools discussed in these pages. This book is a clarion call to individuals and society as a whole to embrace the tools; to esteem a set of core moral and spiritual values; and to live by them, resulting in more peace, happiness, productivity and civility.

When Gandhi said, *"Be the change you wish to see in the world,"* and when Christ said, *"You are the light of the world"* (Matthew 5:14), they were making the same point that this book highlights: you will make the world a better place if you make yourself a better person.

Though reading about the tools is an important first step, the real value comes with incorporating them into your everyday experience. You must daily ask yourself the question: What's in my toolbox? As you answer that question, don't forget to confer with your divine consultant: "Unless the LORD builds the house, the builders labor in vain" (Psalm 127:1).

Two metaphors permeate this book: building a house; taking a journey. Each day you use the tools is both a step forward and a cornerstone laid. You may experience success, fulfillment and inspiration on that day; you may not. But rest assured: positive outcomes will come—sometimes unexpectedly; often spectacularly—as you diligently and faithfully apply the tools. Live according to the ten touchstones and your life will become a steady, unending series of hurdles overcome, adversities vanquished, goals attained, dreams realized and destiny fulfilled. Inspiration, in other words, will actually become not a point in time, something that comes and goes, a one-shot deal . . . but will be *the* distinguishing feature of your day to day life—all of your life.

Your example will shine like the sun through ordinary acts of everyday love.

And best of all, your new way of living, and of being, will inspire someone—family, friend or even stranger—to reach for the glory.

ACKNOWLEDGMENTS

This book would not be possible without the perseverance and guidance of my agent, Cynthia Manson, and the cultivation and insight of my editor, Christine Pride. The support of friends and mentors was also invaluable, especially the spiritual sustenance rising from ministers at my church Bethel Gospel Assembly: Bishop Carlton Brown, Associate Pastor Gordon Williams, Rev. Mimsie Robinson and Elder Vincent Williams. The devotion of my beloved sister, Lucy, and her husband, Robert, has been a cornerstone of this literary work. And last but certainly not least, my greatest thanks goes to the Lord God Almighty—my Provider and Deliverer—of Whose glorious design this book prays to be a part.

ABOUT THE AUTHOR

Photo courtesy of Joseph Holland

Joseph Holland is a community-based entrepreneur, attorney, writer, and ordained minister with more than thirty years experience working at the grassroots level in law, business, community service, and government. He earned a bachelor's degree and a master's degree from Cornell University, where he was an All-American football player, and holds a law degree from Harvard Law School. Holland has received numerous awards and honors for both his business and social-service accomplishments. In 1993, President Bill Clinton recognized him at a White House event for his community-building initiatives. Stemming from his work with the homeless, Holland founded Holistic Hardware, a life-skills program, and cofounded the Beth-Hark Christian Counseling Center. His spiritual memoir, *From Harlem with Love: An Ivy Leaguer's Inner-City Odyssey*, was published in 2012. His first play, *Cast Me Down*, enjoyed an off-Broadway run; and his second play, *Homegrown*, experienced two extended runs at Harlem's National Black Theatre.